Memories *of a* VIETNAM VETERAN

What I Have Remembered and
What He Could Not Forget

by
Barbara Child

 CHIRON PUBLICATIONS • ASHEVILLE, NORTH CAROLINA

www.ChironPublications.com

Interior and cover design by Danijela Mijailovic
Printed primarily in the United States of America.

ISBN978-1-63051-691-8 paperback
ISBN978-1-63051-692-5 hardcover
ISBN978-1-63051-693-2 electronic
ISBN978-1-63051-694-9 limited edition paperback

Library of Congress Cataloging-in-Publication Data

Names: Child, Barbara, 1938- author.
Title: Memories of a Vietnam veteran : what I have remembered and what he could not forget / by Barbara Child.
Description: Asheville, N.C. : Chiron Publications, [2018] | Includes bibliographical references and index.
Identifiers: LCCN 2018059629| ISBN 9781630516918 (pbk. : alk. paper) | ISBN 9781630516925 (hardcover : alk. paper)
Subjects: LCSH: Child, Barbara, 1938- | Morris, Alan George, 1949-1996. | Vietnam War, 1961-1975--Veterans--Florida--Gainesville--Biography. | United States. Army. Medical Detachment, 57th--Biography. | Post-traumatic stress disorder--Patients--United States--Biography. | Man-woman relationships. | Suicide victims--United States--Biography. | Veterans--United States--Social conditions--20th century. | Vietnam War, 1961-1975-- Social aspects--United States. | Unitarian Universalist Association--Clergy--Biography. | Woman seminarians--California--Berkeley--Biography. | Vietnam War, 1961-1975--Personal narratives, American.
Classification: LCC DS559.73.U6 C46 2018 | DDC 616.85/2100922 [B] --dc23
LC record available at https://lccn.loc.gov/2018059629

"Barbara Child's poignant memoir *Memories of a Vietnam Veteran* shares the intimate stories of a combat medic and a home front peace activist during and after their wars at home and overseas. We learn how both were indelibly reshaped by the horrors of that war. Through their stories we learn the impact that war had not just on veterans but every one of us who lived through the era. *Memories* documents this courageous search to heal and find soul's peace. Barbara Child reveals, with gentleness, insight, courage and truly undying love, that the country we dwell in is the human heart, that our beloveds are with us, we tend them forever, and the relationship endures beyond death and can bring forth unexpected new growth."

Edward Tick, Ph.D., author of *War and the Soul* and *Warrior's Return* and director of Soldier's Heart, Inc.

"I find the writing marvelous. [The book] is wonderfully written, and I really would like to see it out in the world."

Jonathan Shay, Veterans Administration psychiatrist and author of *Achilles in Vietnam: Combat Trauma and the Undoing of Character* and *Odysseus in America: Combat Trauma and the Trials of Homecoming*

"This beautifully written memoir succeeds on any number of levels....The chronicle of Barbara Child's time (at Kent State) with and apart from Alan Morris, adds to the public record of the aftermath of the 1970 shootings. Her personal stories add much more to what is known about lives spent in Vietnam as well as in post-1970 Kent, Ohio."

Thomas M. Grace, author of *Kent State: Death and Dissent in the Long Sixties*

"Barbara Child's book...is beautifully written, with compelling material that is as applicable today as it was then. Only the terrain of the wars changes."

Margaret O. Ryan, Senior Editor, *Psychological Perspectives, a Quarterly Journal of Jungian Thought*

"Barbara Child has given us the moving and desperate reality of her life as a partner of a Vietnam vet. In this story of a dust-off medic who could not allow himself to forget, yet would not articulate what he had seen during hundreds of hours of combat assault, we are brought up short against the dehumanizing consequences of war."

Laura Waterman, author of *Losing the Garden: The story of a Marriage*

"*Memories of a Vietnam Veteran* chronicles Barbara Child's journey to wholeness, examining her life and that of her partner Alan, a combat medic who committed suicide 26 torturous years after returning from Vietnam. As a detective might piece together a crime scene, Child follows the threads of her psyche-soma and external evidence to piece together Alan's life *and hers* through memories, dreams, and reflections, along with social justice activism, her Unitarian Universalist ministry, Taoism, depth psychology, and grief rituals. As she quotes the poet Wendell Berry, 'The impeded stream is the one that sings.' And indeed it does."

Arnie Kotler, coeditor with Maxine Hong Kingston, *Veterans of War, Veterans of Peace*

Dedicated
to the memory of

Alan George Morris

Born Newcastle, England
January 10, 1949

Died Fort White, Florida, USA
May 17, 1996

and also dedicated to

Thomas Elsner

Preface

Nearly 25 years ago I wrote a letter to my partner, Alan, while we were at opposite ends of the country. He was at the cottage we shared on the Santa Fe River in North Florida, and I was away at school in Berkeley, California. Alan was a Vietnam War veteran, and I was taking a seminary course on war—in particular, the Vietnam War. I decided to turn in my letter to Alan as a term paper for the course, so I gave it a title, "An Open Letter to a Vietnam Veteran." A little more than two years later, the war finally took its toll on Alan. He put a Colt .45 to his head and pulled the trigger. I read part of my Open Letter as the eulogy at his memorial service.

My Open Letter, written all those years ago, led to one thing, then another, and finally to my writing this book. I never expected to write such a book. However, a couple of years ago, I began analysis with a Jungian psychologist. To introduce him to various important things about my life I shared with him some of my writings, including the Open Letter. In our sessions, I found myself talking more and more about Alan. And I wrote more and more about Alan. From those writings came this book.

Part One is a memoir of my decade with Alan—the last decade of his tortured life. It is also an up-close, partner's-eye view of post-traumatic stress and moral injury as they take their toll on the body, mind, and soul of a veteran who served as a medic in the Vietnam War. My Open Letter, included in full in Chapter 2, recounts some of those experiences. Alan and I talked about writing a book together to expose some often-hidden truths about war and its effects on people. He recorded some of his most haunted memories. These writings—in his own words—are woven into Part One.

This book is more than a memoir, however. It is also a case study of Jungian analysis. In other words, it is a study of how dream work with an expert, caring analyst can bring forth memories and the meaning of memories both sought and unsought. That is the focus of Part Two.

I hope you will experience this book as my labor of love in memory of Alan. I hope you will also hear it as my *cri de coeur*, my impassioned outcry and protest on behalf of all victims of war, whatever their part in the suffering. Finally, I hope you will share my amazement and even delight in the often surprising gifts of dreams, especially dreams shared with a wise and compassionate analyst.

Author's Note

Not long into writing this book, I began to ask myself what Alan would think of other people reading it—the story of our years together, the story of his living and dying as a veteran of the Vietnam War.

I remembered our conversations about writing a book together to document what he knew of that war. I have pages full of his angular block print almost etched into the paper by his ball point pen as he slammed down memory after memory, horror after horror. He had been

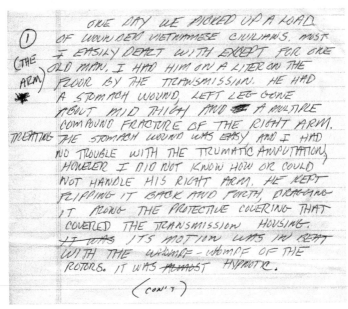

Some of Alan's writing about his memories.

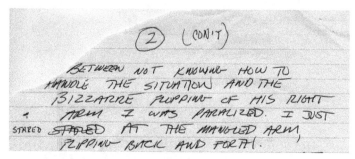

Some of Alan's writing about his memories.

a "dust-off" medic. "Dust-off" was the nickname for the Huey medevac helicopter, "derived from the radio call sign given to the 57th Medical Detachment … evacuation unit in Vietnam (1962) and stands for Dedicated, Unhesitating Support To Our Fighting Forces." (https://www.claybakerdustoff.org/home) "[D]ust-off aircraft suffered 3.3 times more losses to hostile fire than all other forms of helicopter missions. But by the end of the war, some 390,000 South Vietnamese military and civilian patients, U.S. allies, and U.S. personnel had been evacuated by helicopter to a medical facility. Without the skill, devotion, and bravery of the dust-off crews, the number of American dead would have been significantly higher." (Chinnery, 1994)

As a dust-off medic, Alan had been lowered by helicopter, over and over again, his position lighted by flares, to pick up wounded men or dead bodies, or parts of bodies, one at a time. He recorded his memories for two purposes: for the book we planned to write, and to serve as what the Veterans Administration called "stressor letters," which were required to substantiate claims for PTSD [Post-Traumatic Stress Disorder] benefits. Here is the introductory letter Alan wrote to the VA:

Dear Sir:

It has come to my attention that it is beneficial for one who is filing a claim for PTSD to include "stressor" letters. As a dust-off medic I flew hundreds of hours of combat assault. I suffered enough stressful experiences to fill a book. I find it very difficult to even think about the several stories that follow, let alone to write about them.

I was subject to a few incidents that were much, much worse than any that I am presenting here. I have struggled all my adult life to not even think about them and I certainly cannot talk or write about them. I hope that what I have included is enough to make my point.

Alan Morris

Surely it would be all right with him for me to describe what it was like for him to live as a Vietnam veteran plagued by the ravages of that war. He would want others to understand the reality behind what gets inadequately labeled "PTSD," its flashbacks, hyper-vigilance, and the need to be numb, anesthetized, in one way or another—dead. He would want others to know the truths about war as he knew them. Yet Alan was a very private person. He rarely talked about his experiences in Viet Nam or what it felt like to live as a veteran of that war. He rarely talked about himself at all. In fact, he was generally not much of a talker. Would he be horrified by my exposing, over two decades after his suicide, what he had kept to himself? I cannot know. His reaction might include both pride and horror, though finally I believe he would be willing to stifle the horror if others could learn from the truths of his life and death. I record here his memories, in his own words, along with mine.

In the Open Letter I wrote him a couple of years before his death, I told him I understood I could not tell his story; I could tell only mine. In this book, I tell as much of his story as I know how to tell. I also tell my story.

I will give any proceeds I receive from the sale of this book to Veterans for Peace. According to their Mission and Statement of Purpose, they are "an international organization made up of military veterans, military family members, and allies . . . dedicated to building a culture of peace, exposing the true costs of war, and healing the wounds of war." (www.veteransforpeace.org)

Barbara Child
Nashville, Indiana
July 31, 2016

Prologue

Agents Provocateurs

Alan Morris and I met on the campus of Kent State University in 1972. I was on the English Department faculty, and I was also teaching a non-credit course on civil liberties through the Honors College. Civil liberties were much on our minds those days at Kent State. On May 4, 1970, four Kent State students had been killed and nine more wounded by the Ohio National Guard during a demonstration against the escalation of the Vietnam War. At the time of the killings, I chaired the Board of the Portage County chapter of the American Civil Liberties Union. First Amendment rights of free speech and assembly figured so much in our work that I taught the civil liberties course so students could have a deeper understanding of their rights and how best to protect them. Alan Morris took the class.

It turned out that Alan had more than one reason for being in that class. He was one of the founding leaders of the Kent chapter of Vietnam Veterans Against the War (VVAW). He and co-leader Ken Johnson had a growing suspicion that the Kent VVAW had in their midst an agent provocateur, an undercover member of the KSU police force. Alan and Ken feared that this man was attending their meetings not out of sympathy for their anti-war efforts but to learn the VVAW's protest plans, then subvert them. They feared he might also try to goad the vets into illegal activity and trouble with the law that would render them powerless. Alan asked me whether the ACLU could help expose the man as an agent provocateur.

We could—and did. The ACLU Board met at my house just outside of Kent, and Alan came to a meeting to present the situation. Then he and I met with one of the ACLU's local attorneys. This led to a plan that scared me to death.

Here was the plan. Alan would ask the man, Ron Mohr, if he would sell Alan a Russian AK-47, an illegal weapon that Alan knew Mohr had. If so, Alan would go to his house supposedly to complete the sale and transfer of possession. Meanwhile, the ACLU attorney informed the Kent city police of the place and time of this planned transaction. The police would arrive in time to arrest the would-be seller. There was no love lost between the Kent city police and the KSU police at the time, so the city police were happy to play a role.

The aborted sale of the AK-47 went off as planned. The seller was arrested. Alan Morris was not. Neither did he get shot by either the agent provocateur or the police, which I had come to realize I feared might happen. The VVAW, now free of the agent provocateur, became re-energized. They hatched a plan to invite Daniel Ellsberg to speak at an anti-war rally on the Kent State Commons.

Ellsberg had recently become famous for releasing the Pentagon Papers, the Defense Department's study of U.S. involvement in Viet Nam. He had worked on the study, parts of which came to public attention on the front page of the *New York Times.* (Sheehan, 1971) Senator Mike Gravel read parts of it into the Congressional Record, and the Unitarian Universalist Association's Beacon Press published the multi-volume Gravel Edition. (Gravel, 1971) Little by little, it came to light that U.S. presidents all the way back to Harry Truman in 1945 had misled Congress and the American public about their intentions regarding Viet Nam. We believed our purpose there was to secure an independent, non-Communist South Viet Nam. When President Nixon's bombings of Cambodia, Laos, and the North Vietnam Coast came to light, we learned that the true aim was to contain China. (FitzGerald, 2002).

Ellsberg was charged with conspiracy, espionage, and theft of government property. He insisted that his aim in releasing the Pentagon Papers was to expose the lies of a series of American presidents, and to end the wrongful war the U.S. was waging in Southeast Asia. (Ellsberg, 2002) The charges were dropped after it was revealed that the Nixon government had ordered unlawful efforts to discredit Ellsberg, including raiding the files in his psychiatrist's office. The Kent State University community rejoiced when the U.S. Supreme Court vindicated the publication of the Pentagon Papers in *New York Times v. United States*, 403 U.S. 713 (1971).

When the public learned about Nixon's incursion into Cambodia, the Kent State anti-war protests went into high gear. The National Guard killings took place the following Monday, May 4, 1970. It is significant to the Kent community that the National Archives and Records

Administration chose an anniversary of the May 4 date to announce in 2011 that the entire Pentagon Papers would be declassified and released.

In the fall of 1972, government surveillance of anti-war protestors was much on the minds of the VVAW and the ACLU. The organizations jointly invited Daniel Ellsberg to speak at Kent State, and he accepted.

It was one of the best attended anti-war rallies ever on our campus. From their previous experience with the agent provocateur, the VVAW suspected there were others among the many undercover government and police people at the rally. Coincidentally, I knew of one undercover agent of the Kent State police who would be there. The rally with Daniel Ellsberg was designed, in part, to expose such people. We employed the same techniques the authorities did. We scattered a number of spotters in the crowd. I located the man I knew was an undercover agent. When he moved, I watched to see whom he talked to. One of our spotters then watched that man to see whom he talked to. And on it went. By the end of the rally we had a full collection of snapshots to put on display at the next ACLU meeting.

As ACLU Board chair, I was honored to introduce Daniel Ellsberg at the rally on the Commons. A picture taken while I was speaking shows Ellsberg behind me, watching the watchers. Also on stage were Benson Wolman, Executive Director of Ohio ACLU, and, wearing his usual Army fatigues and representing the VVAW, Alan Morris.

By this time, I had gotten to know Alan a little better. After the ACLU Board meeting in my living room,

Introducing Daniel Ellsberg on the Kent State University Commons, October 4, 1972. Photograph by George B. Wuerthele.

he asked if he might come out and fish in the pond beyond my deck. I would see him out there for long stretches, fishing pole in hand, standing motionless. He never came to my door or announced his presence. We never spoke. Yet even without looking, I always somehow knew when he was there.

After the Ellsberg rally I lost track of Alan. He left Kent sometime after my class on civil liberties ended. I had no reason to notice when he left or where he went. I found out only many years later that he had graduated with a B.A. degree in 1977. But at the time I was busy with transitions in my own life. My ACLU work in the wake of the Kent killings moved me slowly out of my identity as an English professor and into the world of law, first as a practicing Legal Aid attorney, then directing writing programs and teaching in law schools. I moved from Kent to San Francisco in 1981 and then, in 1985, to Gainesville, Florida. One fine day during the summer of 1986, well over a decade after I had last seen him, Alan Morris called me, asked if he could come to visit, and then appeared in my office. And it came to pass that in time and in his own way, Alan Morris turned out to be a different sort of agent of provocation.

Table of Contents

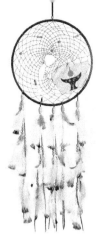

Part One

A Lifetime Is Too Narrow to Understand It All

Chapter *1*

Living in Florida

a lifetime is too narrow
to understand it all, beginning with the huge
rockshelves that underlie all that life.

....

But there come times – perhaps this is one of them –
when we have to take ourselves more seriously or die;
when we have to pull back from the incantations,
rhythms we've moved to thoughtlessly,
and disenthrall ourselves, bestow
ourselves to silence, or a deeper listening....

—Adrienne Rich
from "Transcendental Etude"

When Alan Morris unexpectedly called me out of
nowhere that summer in 1986, I could not have been
more surprised. After renting for a year, I had just
bought a house in Gainesville and moved into it. My
mind was on unpacking and getting ready for the new
school year. Alan Morris, eh? Well, sure I would be
happy to see him, I said. He would be a distraction, I

thought ...but what on earth would we have to say to each other?

But then I had a flash of memory of him out there fishing in the pond at my place outside of Kent. And another flash of him at the front of our anti-war marches at KSU, holding up one end of the VVAW banner with Ken Johnson on the other end. The truth was that I had loved watching him, the swagger in his walk, the jut of his chest, and the set of his jaw. And so now I said, yes, I would be happy to see him. He should come to Gainesville to visit me. And suddenly, there he was.

My office that year was the former kitchen in a former apartment on the second floor of an old house across the street from the law building. We called the place Wilbur Hall, named for the owner of the old house and the little convenience store in front of it. To reach our Legal Drafting Department offices on the second floor of Wilbur Hall, you came up an outside stairway from the parking lot in the back. I could sit at my desk and see who was coming up those stairs. That Friday afternoon, Alan Morris was coming up the stairs.

It was near the end of the day, and I thought we would go to my house and sit on the screened porch and catch up on all those years since we had last seen each other. But I wasn't sure whether either of us really cared about doing that. To tell the truth, I wasn't sure what he was doing there or why I had agreed he should come. He didn't want to go directly to my house. We should go have a drink somewhere first, he said. I had drink fixings at my house, I said. We could have drinks there. No, he said. First, what he wanted to do was have a drink at some bar.

I picked a bar downtown on University Avenue, the place where we met often after that on Friday afternoons when he drove up from Ponce Inlet, near Daytona Beach, where he lived.

That first Friday afternoon, when enough rum and cokes ("cocktails," he called them) had relaxed him enough to be able to have a conversation, he told me about the sleuthing that led to his finding me. He had driven up from Florida to Kent, to Water Street, home of Kent's then famous blues music scene. He knew how I loved blues, and he also knew I had spent some time in the mid-1970s in a relationship with a guitar player in one of the Water Street blues bands. If that guitar player was still there, he might know what had become of Barbara Child, who was clearly no longer in Kent. The guitar player was still there, and he told Alan he had heard I was in Florida, teaching in one of the law schools. Alan called Florida State in Tallahassee first. No luck. His second call bore fruit. There I was, at the University of Florida in Gainesville. He called me. And then he came to see me.

And first thing, we tanked up at a bar on University Avenue. He really couldn't do anything else, I came to discover, until he tanked up. I didn't need those drinks quite that much, at least not in the beginning, not as much as he did, but I put away a fair amount of bourbon that Friday afternoon. It made everything that followed easier.

And so our relationship began, a relationship that changed in major ways over the next decade, which is to say, over the rest of Alan's life. But in the beginning, there was a fair amount of what at least seemed like light-heartedness in it, even gaiety. Alan had brought his mother, Enid, down from Cuyahoga Falls, Ohio, where she had lived for years, and they had a house in Ponce Inlet. Alan had worked for a while with the famous diver Mel Fisher, retrieving coins and other treasure from sunken Spanish ships off the coast of Florida. He taught school for a while as a substitute in industrial arts education. He worked for a guy taking people out on fishing expeditions. Nothing you could call a profession. Nothing for very long.

Alan's life was in most ways completely different from mine. Even though I had changed professions a couple of times over the years, my work was always professional. I was a solid citizen, you could say. When I drank, it was usually at a faculty party or at home, almost never at a bar.Alan hung out a lot in one beach bar or another. When I visited him in Ponce Inlet, I saw firsthand how well known he was to all the regulars along the beach. I'm sure one of the things that attracted me to him was his *not* being a solid citizen. I lived one life during the week, wearing my proper law faculty suit and teaching people how to follow a whole lot of legal drafting rules. And on weekends I hung out with Alan.

Soon enough, stopping at a bar on the way home from the law school became unnecessary. We drank at the table on my back porch, or in my hot tub. We danced naked around the bedroom to the music of Joe Cocker ("Do I still figure in your life?") and Jimmy Buffett. I especially liked Joe Cocker because his pronunciation of "figure" as "figur" was one of the few British pronunciations Alan had retained from his early childhood. Maybe that mattered to me because my heritage is partly English too. My father was born in London. And just as my grandfather brought my father to this country as a very young boy, Alan's mother brought him here when he was very young.

In the early years of my time with Alan in Florida, anyone who saw us would surely have thought this was an idyllic relationship. We went to the Alachua County Fair that first fall and went into the photo booth where the pictures of us show Alan tickling me and both of us having a grand time. We went to a picnic at Cedar Key on

In the photo booth at the Alachua County (Florida) Fair, Fall 1986.

At a picnic at Cedar Key, Florida, late 1980's.

the Gulf, and somebody took a picture of us sitting at a picnic table. In the picture I am evidently teasing Alan about something, giving him a gentle poke in the arm. He is evidently getting a kick out of it. By that time, he had cleaned himself up for some job or other, gotten his hair cut, and bought a reasonable car to drive back and forth from Ponce Inlet to Gainesville.

Still, it was about that time that there came a Friday evening when I began to worry because it was getting later and later and Alan had not arrived. Well, I would have a drink and he would be there soon. Finally, he called. He was in the Marion County jail. He was that close to Gainesville, just about 45 miles from my house, when he was arrested for DUI. He wanted me to come and bail him out. Oh my. The trouble was that by that time, I was quite drunk myself. Was I actually going to drive to Ocala and deal with a bail bondsman and the deputies at the jail besides? Could I manage all this without getting myself arrested? But there was really no question in my mind about what I would do. I would go to the Marion County jail in Ocala and bail Alan out. And I did. I do not remember our ride up to Gainesville. I'm sure it was not a happy one. Nor could have been our ride back down to Ocala the next day for him to retrieve his car from the impound lot.

***

The year 1988 was monumental in my life. I turned fifty that year, the first edition of my legal drafting textbook was published, my menopause came and went, and I had to have a lump in my right breast biopsied. I was terrified, almost as much of disfigurement as of cancer. It turned out I did not have cancer, and the surgeon who took a chunk out of my breast was so skillful that to this day, unless I raise my arm above my head, it's impossible to tell what happened then.

But what I remember most about that whole episode was how grateful I was for Alan's presence in my life. When I came out of the anesthesia that day, there he was. There he was to be with me when the surgeon came in to give me the initial pathology report, whatever that report would have to say. And in the days that followed when I still could not bear to look at my own wounded body, there he was to change the dressings. Alan had been a medic in Viet Nam. He knew how to do these things. He knew how to be with a wounded person.

> Some of my earliest stressful experiences occurred early in my tour while assigned to the 7th Surgical Hospital at Blackhorse Base Camp (11th Armored Cavalry Regiment) near Xuan Loc, IV Corps, under the overall command of (then) Col. George S. Patton III. I was only there a couple of months and I was assigned as a medic on a post-op ward in a unit that was very, very much like the popular T.V. series "M.A.S.H." Occasionally we would get hit hard, meaning many incoming dust-offs carrying many more casualties than we were equipped to handle. Often dozens more! I vividly remember row upon row upon pile upon

pile of dead and wounded laying out in the dusty, blistering hot environment while we would do triage.

As the doctors and nurses chose those to be carried off to the O/R I was left to load body bags with various body parts (hands, arms, heads, legs, feet, torsos, etc.) and sometimes even a rather intact corpse. We would stash them in a large steel conEx [storage container] until they were removed, by I don't know who. I did not care for this type of activity.

Once while on the post-op ward, during night shift, a senior N.C.O. was required to do a "special" and I was his assistant. This meant constant care of a patient who was not expected to make it till morning. He was a large black male with no arms and no legs. The only thing showing was what was left of his head and the rest was bandages, I.V.'s, tubes, etc. We had him tied to the back of the bed in an upright position and he was struggling, and screaming constantly. Fortunately (for me) he did some projectile vomiting which hit me. I was covered with green vomit that looked like very thin green pea soup, but had an odor so putrid that I cannot describe it. Since I was a mess, I was allowed to leave to shower and change. During my absence I was replaced.

Another time on the same post-op ward, I was required to assist another senior N.C.O.

in a dressing change. The guy was laying on his stomach as most of the tissue on the back of his calves and thighs was missing. My job was to hold up one leg at a time while Sgt. B____ un-wrapped the bandages. The guy's screaming in agony was so horrible that I let the first leg slip. Sgt. B_____ yelled at me, "Morris, get your shit together." I did. I was able to assist in the dressing changes and irrigation of both legs while this guy screamed in agony non-stop. After it was over and he was through crying, he said to me something to the effect of "If I could move and fight I would not have let you guys do that to me."

This made me feel very guilty even though our procedures were meant to try to save his legs. I would be surprised if he still has them. I can still hear his screams to this very day.

Something else of importance to me happened that year. After about thirty years of steadily escalating addiction to alcohol, I stopped drinking. It was, of course, anything but easy. I went to see an addictions counselor by the name of Diane Rogers. I credit her with saving my life. I went to see her, I said, on account of Alan's drinking. I told her he suffered so mightily from post-traumatic stress related to the war that he had himself anesthetized pretty much all the time. I was worried for his health, I told her, but for another reason too. He insisted on keeping a loaded pistol on the floor by his side of the bed every night. Well, I was just worried, that was all.

Diane Rogers began asking me questions, natural ones, I thought, to get the lay of the land. What did Alan drink? How early in the day did he start? Did I have a drink with him? I answered her questions, and ever so slowly she managed to get beyond what amounted to my cover story, that I was there on account of Alan's drinking. Diane Rogers was a smart woman. She was able to weave a thread that ensnared me. I agreed to write down exactly what I drank, and how much and when, every single day. I could drink as much as I wanted, only I had to keep my agreement to record every drink.

By this time, I had begun to believe that some people in high places in the law school were undermining my Legal Drafting Program, which they had not really wanted to have in the first place. They maintained that new attorneys could learn "skills," which they mentioned in a derisive tone of voice, apprenticing in a law office. The proper province of the law school, these senior faculty members thought, was exclusively the substance of the law. When the Legal Drafting Program began, there was an agreement that it would be reviewed in its third year with the intention to decide whether it should continue. This program was my progeny, the fruit of my spirit. The instructors I had trained depended on me for their professional reputation as well as their livelihood. I could not let them or the program down. I had to be fully on deck if we were going to survive the three-year review. I knew that. At the same time, I knew I was getting up every morning with a splitting headache and, just like Alan, drinking myself every evening into a stupor.

Alan said I was having blackouts. He said it was too bad I had a drinking problem and it was probably a good thing I was getting some kind of help, but he wasn't getting any help because he didn't care if he drank too much, or even if it would kill him. He was living on borrowed time anyway, he said. He was a crazy Vietnam vet, he said, who was home because of a bullet that took out the medic on the other end of a litter and blew the head off the guy they were loading onto the chopper. Somehow, that bullet only took off a piece of Alan's thigh as it sped between his legs after taking out the guy on the litter and the medic at the other end.

I began to think about what it might be like to quit drinking. I began to think that, yes, someday I was going to have to do that. Most people, law school colleagues and friends alike, had no idea I was an alcoholic. A law school is an easy place to develop that addiction. Put together the stress of academic politics and flowing high end booze, and it's a natural.

At one point, I decided that Diane Rogers had done everything she could do for me, or rather I didn't really need therapy anymore. I had learned everything there was for me to learn, and besides, she wasn't all that good anyway. She didn't have all the answers. The couple of friends who knew what was going on leaned on me heavily. I would never be able to quit drinking, they said, if I stayed with Alan. And suddenly a response came from somewhere deep inside of me. "Watch me," I said. I had my last drink on September 20, 1988, and I stayed with Alan.

Our relationship did change after I quit drinking, but I attributed that to his PTSD.

For whatever reason, the Cav. was moved up north and our 7th Surgical Hospital was disbanded. I was then assigned to a dispensary at some enormous base camp. It may have been Long Binh; I don't recall. I do however remember that for the first time in my Army career I was without anyone that I had started with (basic, A.I.T., Rangers, Stateside, 7th Surg.). I had never felt so lonely and lost in my entire life. My duty was to handle sick call, which consisted of one or two hundred guys a day. Most of them had absolutely nothing wrong with them. I found this to be very boring. I felt useless, and combined with the severe loneliness, depression, and isolation I was experiencing, I knew I had to get a transfer even after only having been there a few weeks. The only way for a medic to get a transfer from that unit at that time was to volunteer to fly dust-off. I discussed this with two of the doctors I worked with who were both vets of the 101st Airborne Division. They laughed at me and advised me that I was better off to stay put, as the last thing they said I needed to do was fly dust-off. I persisted with my request, they told me I was nuts to leave a secure job in a secure base camp, but finally agreed to let me go. I passed my flight physical and was assigned to the 4th Platoon, 45th Air Ambulance Company. I was soon to learn why they had so strongly advised me against doing so.

Sometimes when there was no L/Z [landing zone] we would have to hoist. This was a ship rigged with a hydraulically controlled steel cable & tipped with a J/P [Jungle Penetrator]. It was designed to crash through even triple-canopy jungle. It had seats that unfolded so that the wounded could be strapped on & hoisted to the ship. We had one ship rigged in this manner at all times & we rotated this duty. It was a great way to get wasted; hovering directly in the tree tops for long periods of time. I'll never forget M_____ & J_____, who took a direct hit with an R.P.G. while hoisting. They burned, crashed, & died. I especially disliked hoist missions.

My last mission that I was allowed to fly was out of Tan An, on or about 7 Sept. '69. It started out as a rather routine mission although it was at night and in a rather bad A/O [Area of Operation], a place called the Plain of Reeds. But the folks on the ground hadn't had contact in two weeks and the patient had F.U.O. [Fever of Unknown Origin]. We landed and since he wasn't ambulatory I jumped out with a litter, and myself and

MEMORIES OF A VIETNAM VETERAN

the ground medic loaded him on the litter. I then started backing up as I carried the guy with the other medic walking forward at the other end of the litter facing me.

Suddenly snipers opened up with AK's. They were very close in the tall elephant grass. I could see bullets coming through the other medic and the guy on the litter. As this occurred their forward motion from the hits pushed me backwards against the chopper, which was already in the process of taking off. I ended up laying on my back, head first, half on and half off the bouncing chopper as the pilot tried to gain some control. The crew chief drug me on board, saving my life. We were bouncing and shaking and flipping side to side. I don't know how many hits we had taken but the ship looked like Swiss cheese. Some of the fuel cells had been shot up and we were leaking JP-4 [jet fuel] into the cockpit real bad. It was sloshing around about 2 or 3 inches deep, so we opened all the doors so it could run out. I was completely soaked in JP-4 and was terrified that we were all going to be incinerated.

After a few moments I felt this terrible burning sensation on my right upper & lower leg. This is when I realized that I was hit as the aviation fuel was soaking my wounds and burning like hell.

I patched myself up, the pilot put out a Mayday to include that his medic was hit, and somehow continued to fly and gain altitude. Gas was still pouring everywhere. One of my biggest fears in combat had always been getting burned up. I figured that my time had come so I got right at the edge of the open door and decided that at the first flash of fire I would jump to my death rather than burn up. That flash never came and it was one wild ride but somehow the A/C [Aircraft Commander] flew that gas can full of holes back to Tan An and landed safely. We never did catch on fire.

We went into the aid station and I jumped up on a litter while the surgeons checked me out. I had relatively minor wounds, no bones, arteries, nerves, just "flesh wounds" like a John Wayne cowboy movie.

About this time, we encountered in-coming mortars, big ones. Everyone hit the floor. I stayed/sat upright on the litter and merely covered my ears with my hands. (I hated and was scared by loud gun fire and explosions.) Everyone on the floor looked up at me like I was crazy. I guess that by this time I had seen a bit too much action and was more concerned about loud noises than my personal safety. (To this day I suffer from startle reaction and cannot stand to even be in a room where balloons are present—such as a party.) The last one incoming hit the hooch we were in and blew out a large section of the tin roof. None of us was hit and everyone got back up.

No sooner had they done so than we got hit with a ground attack. Once again everyone hit the deck and assumed defensive positions and I just sat there on the litter with my hands shielding my ears from the noise. It must not have been much of an attack because it didn't last long. I guess the guys on the perimeter got 'em all.

People started carrying in the wounded and about this time a dust-off from my platoon arrived to rescue my crew; we boarded and split back to our rear area.

I think everyone on that mission deserved a medal but I have no idea if they got one because I never saw any of them again. (I did later receive a Purple Heart for taking the two hits.)

First thing next morning I was ordered to report to Sgt. So & So at 93rd Evac Hospital which was located a short walk just across our flight line. This seemed a bit odd to me but I complied.

Sgt. So & So was obviously a medic psych. type & he asked me questions and took notes. After a bit of this he said I needed to go & see the colonel down the hall. I did and the col. was a psychiatrist. He started asking more questions and also taking notes. Apparently, some of the doctors and other personnel had found my behavior during the previous day's firefights a bit odd. I don't recall all that was discussed but I do remember his last words. They went something like this: "Young man, you've seen too much combat; enough is enough. I'm grounding you and you're out of your unit. No more combat for you! Sgt. So & So will drive you to 24th Evac Hospital."

***

Though Alan and I spent a lot of time in the hot tub on my back porch in Gainesville, we both longed for a place on water. I dreamed of a place on a lake, a place where I could go swimming right out the front door as I remembered doing during some of the best parts of my childhood. He said it was silly to think about swimming in a Florida lake because it was sure to harbor alligators. Alan dreamed of a place on a river. You could go boating on a river, he said. Besides, one river usually emptied into another, so from a place on a river, you might be able to get to anywhere in the world.

We started looking. We often went on weekend excursions to look at cabins or cottages on some body of water. I looked at some lake places when he wasn't along, probably because I knew he would find some reason to rule them out. And in the end, the river cottage we picked appealed to me just as much as it did him. It was a simple little cement block cottage on the Santa Fe River northwest of Gainesville, a couple of miles outside of a little town called Fort White. It had a

The cottage on the Santa Fe River, near Fort White, Florida.

screened-in porch, and you only had to walk a little way down hill in the yard from the porch to reach the dock.

You couldn't swim in the Santa Fe because of alligators, but that had its advantages too. The alligators were there because they liked the tannic water. The water was tannic because of the cypress swamp on the other side of the river, just a couple of hundred feet away. And because of the cypress swamp, nobody would ever be able to build on the land over there. We could enjoy that beautiful view knowing it would never be disturbed. Also, there was a little spring-fed river called the Ichetucknee just walking distance away that emptied into the Santa Fe. Its water was crystal clear, not the least tannic, so there were no alligators there, and I could walk a mile upstream, put myself in the Ichetucknee River, often face down with a snorkel, and swim home.

Much as he liked boating, Alan never went into the river, never swam. But when my swim brought me near the mouth of the Ichetucknee, where it was about to empty into the Santa Fe, there he would be, sitting propped up against a tree with a towel, waiting for me, watching me swim. No doubt about it, the cottage on the Santa Fe was the perfect place for us. And as Alan often mentioned, the Santa Fe emptied into the Suwannee, and the Suwannee emptied into the Gulf of Mexico, and from there you could get to any place in the world.

It was quite okay that the cottage was small, less than 700 square feet, essentially one room plus the bathroom. It was okay that it was made of cement block and had a cement floor. In fact, this was a good thing because the cottage regularly flooded, and this way, you could go in there with bleach and a hose and clean it up pretty quickly. The proximity to the river, and the river view from the porch and nearly every window, made it well worth the floods. The floods were called bathtub

A Santa Fe River flood nearing the cottage.

floods. They happened when the Suwannee flooded and backed up into the Santa Fe. It did this about as slowly as a bathtub backing up, and there was a phone number you could call to get a reading on any day during a flood to let you know the exact level that day, and the date and the number of feet above sea level the flood was expected to crest.

In our case, planning ahead for a flood was a little tricky. We had a big stake planted in the yard with lines on it marking number of feet above sea level. And we came to know that the water entered the cottage through the fireplace before it came through the door. But the really important thing to know was that the access to the cottage from the road would flood before the cottage itself. So, we had to decide when to make the cottage flood-ready and get out of there, even though the cottage might not actually flood that time at all. Making the cottage flood-ready meant slinging the

Rowing down Sante Fe Boulevard to inspect the flooded cottage.

light wicker furniture from hooks in the ceiling, putting small things that could withstand some period of moisture on high shelves, and hauling everything else off to a public storage facility for the duration.

Of course, during a flood we would be enormously curious about how things were at the cottage. When a flood was coming, most people with cottages and the few who had year-round homes there in Three Rivers Estates—about as misnamed as that funky area could possibly be—kept some kind of boat tethered to a tree, near, but safely above where the river was expected to crest. This way, we could go on inspection tours. Once, somebody took a picture of Alan and me rowing down Santa Fe Boulevard past a stop sign on the way to inspect the flooded cottage, and the picture ended up on the front page of the local newspaper. The person from the newspaper must have asked me my name before we rowed off and then must have made an assumption. The caption under the picture in the newspaper referred to "Barbara and Alan Child" taking off to inspect their cottage. Alan was not amused.

Nevertheless, I have remembered our time together in the early 1990s, mostly at the cottage, as a mostly happy time. He had begun working as an account executive for an outdoor advertising company—selling billboard advertising, that is—which gave me some pause, not just on general principles but more specifically because one of his accounts was for Café Risqué, an "adult entertainment establishment," whose billboard made me cringe every time I drove past it on I-75. Nonetheless, I marveled at what an expert salesman Alan was. He did much of his work on the phone, and I would hear him checking in at the office for messages, answering phone calls, following up, taking care of problems. Taking care of business. I never could get over how good he was at it.

He could sell anything—pole barns, billboard ads, jewelry, shark jaws, pistols, Spanish coins known as "pieces of eight." He took to setting up at various outdoor flea markets. I think he could have sold the Brooklyn Bridge if he tried. I used to listen to the tone of his voice on the phone, never hurried, never out of sorts, no matter how he was feeling, no matter what kind of day it had been. "'Preciate it," he would say last thing before he hung up.

That was his work. Alan Morris knew the difference between work and not work. His not work was sitting on the dock fishing, or not fishing. Or taking a quick boat trip upriver from the cottage, up to Crack Rock before the sunset, or checking for the manatee at the mouth of the Ichetucknee, or checking out the spring up by Woodsy G's. Or having a ride in the old blue Ford pick-up to Pope's Store, checking out the Three Rivers neighborhood.

"Come on," he would say, "I want to show you something." And up at the corner of Washington and Idaho Streets, we would sit in the truck in the darkness and silently watch hundreds of fireflies. After a flood there were constant rides. Where was the water today? Had the green slime left Santa Fe Boulevard? Could you get through to Harris Wall's place? Were there any new lots for sale? Had Drew made any progress on the houseboat? Out at Three Rivers there were no end of things to check on always.

It was a life of walks and rides in praise of peace and the beauty of the rivers and the cypress trees, the hawks and the owls, the moonrises and the smell of wood smoke. There was very little talking. With Alan at the river, for the first time in my life, I was able to slow down, sit down, and just be.

I certainly couldn't do that at the law school. In order to secure my position and the Legal Drafting Program itself, I wrote a textbook on drafting legal documents in plain language, which I was thrilled to have published by West Publishing Company, one of the two most highly respected publishers of legal textbooks in the country. During those years while I was spending weekends with Alan at the cottage, I was writing the second edition. I can remember us sitting at the table on the porch, him sucking on a rum and coke and me reviewing page proofs. Whenever I would get tired or discouraged, he would say, "Write that book!" The copy of the second edition that is now on my shelf bears my handwritten inscription, "For Alan with love."

But another transition was underway in my life. Two decades before, even though for years I had loved teaching, when I thought of all the work that needed to be done in the world in the wake of the Kent killings, I had begun to think of my work in the English Department as "fussing with people's commas." And now I was beginning to think of marking law students' papers in about the same way.

One day, Morris Dees, the Director of the Southern Poverty Law Center, came to speak to the University of Florida law students. He had long been a hero of mine, and I was more than a little excited to hear him speak. He was there to urge the students to devote at least some of their time to *pro bono* law. I knew those students. "You are barking up the wrong tree, Morris Dees," I said to myself. And no wonder. As I looked around that auditorium, I noted that very few of my faculty colleagues had seen fit to make time to come to hear Morris Dees speak. He was urging the audience to follow their passions. And I had to acknowledge, at least to myself, that my passion was no longer in the law school.

A new path was opening for me, and that day, Morris Dees helped me see it. I had joined a Unitarian Universalist church in 1963, but after the Kent killings, I rarely went near a church for a very long time. In truth, I was devoted more to the ACLU than to any church. But in Florida, in a law school filled with people whom even the likes of Morris Dees apparently could not inspire to selfless service, I found my way back to church, mainly through the avenue of women's retreats put on by the Women and Religion Committee of the Florida District of the Unitarian Universalist Association. At first, I attended those retreats and later I began to lead some of them. And I began to appreciate the value of religious community as a source of support and meaning in people's lives.

In the summer of 1992, I served on the planning committee for the biennial conference of the Unitarian Universalist Women's Federation. One of the speakers at our conference that June was Rebecca Parker, President of Starr King School for the Ministry, our seminary affiliated with the Graduate Theological Union in Berkeley, California. I took Rebecca Parker out for breakfast one day during the conference. And two months later I sat on the screened porch at the cottage on the Santa Fe River writing my answers to the many essay questions required as part of the application for the Master of Divinity (M.Div.) program at Starr King School.

It would be fair to say that I was not at all sure what I was doing. But one of the wonderful things about Starr King School, something that I know played a part in my applying to study there, is that Starr King does not expect you to know when you walk in the door exactly what you are going to do after you walk back out into the world with your M.Div. degree. In fact—and this is surely still true—Starr King School prefers that you not be too sure about your future in order that you might be open to some transformation during your course of study there.

When I applied, I certainly had no clear intention to become a parish minister. I expected, in a vague sort of way, that I might become some sort of community minister, maybe ministering to addicts, the homeless, veterans. Put another way—ministering to addicted, homeless veterans. In the misnamed Three Rivers Estates area along the Santa Fe River in North Florida, there were a fair number of Vietnam veterans living a fairly minimalist sort of life, essentially survivalists. Alan became buddies after a fashion with some of them. When I mentioned my growing idea about becoming a minister, Alan did not understand what I had in mind, but he had sort of an idea that I might be able to minister to those buddies of his, just barely holding onto some kind of life in the woods of North Florida. He thought that might not be a bad idea. In any case, he never tried to talk me out of going to seminary.

I found out in February of 1993 that I had been accepted and was to begin studying at Starr King School the following September. With the second edition of my legal drafting text in print, I said my goodbyes at the law school—where they gave me a plaque inscribed with some complimentary words and signed by the dean—and sold my house in Gainesville. Alan helped me sell or give away most of my stuff. I rented a studio apartment in Berkeley, sight unseen. We determined that he would live in the cottage on the Santa Fe River while I was gone. We would talk on the phone regularly. I would come home to the cottage for mid-winter breaks and for a month each summer. That's as much as we knew.

At the Grand Canyon in a rain storm, late summer 1993.

But to begin with, he would drive me and what was left of my stuff in a rental truck across the country to Berkeley. And that is what happened. I have several snapshots taken on that trip. The one that has a place in the collection on my dresser, along with the Alachua County Fair snapshots and the picture of us rowing down Santa Fe Boulevard, is a picture Alan took of me at the rim of the Grand Canyon. I am sopping wet with rain, and in the background over the canyon there is barely visible a rainbow.

Chapter 2

An Open Letter to a Vietnam Veteran

> Just as one learns to read and write
> not necessarily to create works of literary art,
> one learns to see like an artist
> not necessarily to create art
> but simply to see and think better.
>
> —Jo Milgrom

That first fall semester at Starr King School, I jumped right in. First thing, I took a course called "Death and Dying." I knew I needed to take that course right away because I needed to discover whether I could actually look at a dead body. I never had, and I wasn't at all sure I could. And if I couldn't, I needed to find that out sooner rather than later. I certainly couldn't become a minister if I couldn't look at a dead body. Better to find that out right away and so save a lot of time and money if I needed to drop out of seminary. I found out I could manage to look, and I stayed.

That fall I also took a course called "Work and Vocation." I needed to learn right away what that course might teach me as well. In fulfillment of one of the requirements of the course, I spent one morning a week down on Telegraph Avenue, so far south it was nearly in Oakland, at a place called the Berkeley Jobs Consortium. Each week, I interviewed a jobless person to find out what kind of experience and skills the person had that might appeal to a potential employer. And then I helped the person write a resume. Help with resume writing was only one of the services the Berkeley Jobs Consortium provided for unemployed people. There was a phone bank. There was a bulletin board with job listings. There were clothes a person could borrow to wear to an interview. I was mightily impressed with the Berkeley Jobs Consortium and deeply moved by my conversations with clients there. Many of them were homeless. More than a few struggled with their attempts at recovery from addiction. And a lot of them were veterans. I got to where I said I could spot a Vietnam veteran a mile away. Well, that was no surprise, sure enough.

That fall, some of my most important learning came in a course I might never have suspected to exist, at least not in the context of seminary education. It was a course on war—war in general and the Vietnam War in particular. This course was offered to Starr King students and others through the Graduate Theological Union. It was taught by Walter Capps, who served in the California legislature and also was a professor of religion at the University of California at Santa Barbara. He had written one book (Capps, 1990) and edited another (Capps, 1991) on the Vietnam War. I couldn't imagine how I could be so lucky as to have Walter Capps and his course on war suddenly drop into my life. Nearly every week, our class meetings featured a visiting speaker, each one with actual experience to share. One week we heard from a nurse who had served in Viet Nam. We heard from several different veterans. One week we heard from someone who worked at a Vet Center—a support organization operating in cities and towns across the country that seemed to me, listening to our visiting speaker, to be serving Vietnam veterans ever so much better than the VA. I vowed to learn whether there was a Vet Center close enough to Gainesville for Alan to get support there. It seemed to me that what he was getting from the VA was just continuing hassle and precious little help.

One of the requirements in Walter Capps' course was to write a term paper. And much as I appreciated both the teaching and the learning in all the other courses I took that first semester in seminary, the experience that I put my heart and soul into was writing that paper. I wrote it as a letter to Alan. And since somebody else, Walter Capps, was going to read it too, since I was going to turn it in to him, I gave it a title— "An Open Letter to a Vietnam Veteran." Alan's birthday was coming up soon, and so the letter was much more than a paper for a course. I was able to give it to him on his birthday.

***

Berkeley, California
January 10, 1994

Dear Alan,

When you gave me Patience Mason's book (Mason, 1990) for Christmas, it seemed to me that you were inviting me into a conversation. Then you flew across the country for New Year's Eve to find out if I'd read it yet. What I wanted you to know was that I had taken Walter Capps' course on the Vietnam War. Your birthday presents on this day, your 45th birthday, are his books on this unfinished war. I hope you will think of this letter as a birthday present too. It does seem, doesn't it, that some conversation has begun—that our silent dance around the war is at last yielding up words, speech, conversation. It is understandable that it has taken this long. Robert Kerrey says of the war that when an event is unspeakable, it takes awhile to find the right words for it.

Still I rejoice as I make this letter part of the beginning conversation. It seemed to me for so long that we were stuck—stuck but not fixed. I never thought of being fixed as a goal. I had no pretentious notions that I could fix the brokenness the war had caused. I wouldn't even want you or us or anybody to be fixed because once fixed, one never moves again. No, what I desire is motion, the reminder that change is still possible. Better yet, that transformation is possible.

I have read of women who write letters to their loved ones who died in the war. They shove their letters in the cracks in the wall at the Vietnam Memorial in Washington. I suppose they may harbor some hope that somehow in spirit their dead will read what they have written. But I think they surely must have more in mind than that. It is surely true that everyone who ever writes a letter to a loved one, dead or alive, writes for the writer's own self first. We discover our thoughts, our feelings, our beliefs in the process of writing. More, we discover who we are. Maybe we even change who we are. But I expect that the women who shove their letters in the cracks in the wall are hoping that other people will take their letters out and read them, and that those people in turn may be touched by them and change.

And as I write this, I am mindful of how lucky I am that I will not be shoving this letter in the wall but giving it to you. If you had died in Vietnam, I would never have met you. I know only a little of the you that you were before the war. Once your mother covered the dining room table with pictures of you, and then she and I walked along the Ponce Inlet beach and she talked about the son she remembered. She grieved mightily that day, and I will always remember it. I heard a poem read this week that was written by a nurse in the Vietnam War. In the poem she says that she did not lose any limbs in the war, but she still grieves some part of her that was left behind in Vietnam, some part that she cannot even identify.

My first memories of you are in Kent when you were first back from the war. I remember you always in fatigues. I remember you at the front of our marches, holding one end of the VVAW banner with Ken Johnson on the other end. I remember you coming out to fish in the pond at my place. It never occurred to me then to think that you were haunted. And yet you had just come back.

In those days I was too busy being haunted myself by the killings at Kent to notice much else. We who were there on the Kent Commons on May 4, 1970, who heard that gunfire, who ran from it, who lived—we were very full of ourselves in those days. Nobody who had not been there could possibly understand, we thought. We talked of nothing else. We thought of nothing else. We were noble in our suffering. We were righteous in our politics. In time we were even sure that it was we who deserved the credit for ending the war. But that was later.

Then, when you showed up in your fatigues with your banner and your swagger and your dark glasses, we welcomed you with open arms. You, after all, were valuable to us. You authenticated our cause. And for myself, I marched tirelessly up the Summit Street hill and past the jeering idiots in the dormitory windows and the honking idiots on Main Street—and I always made sure I was close enough to the front of the march to keep in sight the leaders with the VVAW banner.

I recently heard a story of a nurse from the Vietnam War whose mother promptly threw her fatigues in the trash when she came home. The nurse angrily retrieved them, in spite of her mother's protests that they were tattered and stained and awful to look at. They were her lifeline to the only reality she knew.

I remember that you always wore your fatigues in those days in Kent. I thought it was a political statement, and it probably was in part. But it never occurred to me that you were really still in Vietnam. How silly our mundane concerns about parade permits and regulations on bullhorns must have seemed to you, to say nothing of our perpetual battle with the University administration to get a proper memorial on the campus to the students killed by the National Guard. We were so caught up in the war at home that we often lost sight of the one I now assume you were still living in day and night.

> One time during the day, we picked up a big load (9, 10, or maybe 12) 101st Troopers and 1 A.R.V.N. [Army of the Republic of Vietnam, the South Vietnamese Army]. All were hit by "friendly" fire, probably Cobras or Puff as they were all gunshot wounds. I don't remember where it was, but it must have been way out somewhere, because it was such a long flight back that I had time to get them all stabilized; all, that is, except the A.R.V.N. He was back in the hold—the area where a door gunner would normally man an M-60, except we didn't have any. We carried only personal weapons. One of the Troopers grabbed me and pointed back to the A.R.V.N. He was slumped in the corner and covered with blood, including a very large pool at his feet. I merely made a motion with my finger like slashing my own throat to indicate that he was dead. In fact, I did not know or care. I guess that was part of my racist state-side Ranger experiences: All Vietnamese are bad, "gooks," "kill, kill, kill." We landed at 3rd Field Hospital, were met by

ambulances that immediately whisked away the U.S. grunts. No one touched the A.R.V.N, so I carried him about 50 feet from the chopper and dropped him on the ground and we split. I've often wondered if he was dead or alive. Had he been alive, I quite possibly could have saved his life. I have felt terrible guilt about this incident all my life.

Ironically, we owe it to the war that we ever got together, you and I. There was more than the marches, after all. There were the ACLU meetings at my place and the heady political work of uncovering the agent provocateur in the VVAW. I remember fearing the whole business would backfire and you would be killed. I remember my exhilaration on the platform that day on the Commons introducing Dan Ellsberg, with you sitting behind me, you in your fatigues, of course. That was 1972. You had been home two years then. If there was erotic intensity for me in those few moments of fear and glory, how can I ever claim not to understand your own?

I know that I am frightened in a way that has always mystified me when you are high as a kite on the Fourth of July and want to rock the boat and shoot guns and weave the truck all over the road and howl at the moon. There is nothing mysterious about being afraid of an accident, of course. At those times I want to be as far as I can get from the boat or the truck or wherever you are. The mystery is about what is happening to you then. Whatever it is, it is a force so powerful that it brings you to life. At those moments, you are not numb, frozen, out cold. You are not angry either. You are exhilarated. There is a smile on your face. You want to tease me into laughter, and you want to whoop for joy at your own wildness. And it seems to me that you are very sadly disappointed that what I do then is withdraw. That I don't think the jokes are funny, that to me this play is not a comedy but a drama meant for tears. While you are whooping, I want to cry out for help.

One time we were flying along on a beautiful peaceful day. I don't recall the mission or that we were even on one. When it was slow (no major battles or fire fights) we might fly mail, re-supply, carry nurses to or from parties for the big brass; or even just have a joy ride. This may have been a joy ride as we had no passengers or cargo. I was laid back and relaxed, listening to rock music on Radio Saigon.

I think there were two things that saved our four lives from the crash which we experienced: 1) the relatively high altitude at which we were flying and 2) the skill of the A.C. [Aircraft Commander]

The A.C. hated me and the feeling was mutual. I almost never flew with this A.C. whose name I don't recall although I can picture his face as perfectly as if our last meeting had been yesterday rather than 25 years ago. I don't like him although I will give him credit for saving our lives in the following situation:

Suddenly the transmission made a horrible and extremely loud noise. And then seized. I say loud because flying in a chopper is quite noisy anyway, especially when you're blasting hard rock music through your head sets. About the only thing you can hear above such noise is gunfire and explosions as well as the noise the transmission made during this mechanical failure.

When it locked up we lost complete control of the aircraft; hydraulics etc. We dropped like a rock for a couple thousand feet in seconds. The top of my helmet hit the ceiling with such force that it almost knocked me out. If you have never fallen thousands of feet at approximately 150 m.p.h. with no parachute then you cannot begin to imagine the level of fear experienced.

Somehow the pilot was able to keep us from flipping upside down and then somehow able to regain enough control to sort of auto-rotate and scream out a Mayday. He was able to crash us directly in the center of a rice paddy. His flying skills were worthy of a medal.

None of us were injured so we sloshed as fast as we could to the nearest paddy dike and assumed defensive positions. I had my M-16 and my .38 but left the M-79 grenade launcher I often carried behind.

As I lay in the muddy water I was locked and loaded on full auto with my finger on the trigger, ready for anything that might constitute a threat.

Suddenly a group of Vietnamese civilians appeared on an adjacent dike about 50' away. They were laughing at us hysterically as they pointed at us and jibbered to each other in Vietnamese. I was very unnerved and pissed off. I was just about ready to take them all out (more from rage than self-defense) when the thought occurred that this A.C. hated me anyway and killing the civilians might lead to big trouble. During this instant of hesitation, I heard an incoming Chinook who was obviously responding to our Mayday. He hovered just on the dike and we boarded and split, leaving the civilians alive and still laughing. I consider myself fortunate to have survived the crash and to not be writing this from some federal prison.

As I write this, I hesitate, wondering how on earth you will react when you read it. I find myself wanting to say to you: Wait. Please do not draw conclusions yet. Please do not render judgments now. Please read on. Please understand that I have discovered that I was wrong at the outset when I thought what I would do would be to tell your story, to let you know that I have paid attention to your story, that is, to as much of it as I know, and that, knowing as much as I know, I accept it for what it is.

I have discovered that I cannot tell your story. Only you can do that. The only story I can tell is my own. I have learned this in part from Patience Mason's book about living with her husband, Bob, after he came back from Vietnam. I thank you for introducing me to Bob and Patience in Gainesville, and I thank you for Patience's book. In return, I ask you to be patient with me and in your silence hear my story.

I have listened to your silence for a very long time. Those whooping moments, of course, have been relatively few. More common is the silence. I have grown familiar with it and have communed with it as best I could. At times I have welcomed it, for it has given me the freedom to be with my own thoughts or even sometimes to be without thought. Sometimes I have even called it peaceful. I truly love our silent boat rides and the quiet hours on the dock watching the moon rise behind the cypress trees.

But I have always thought that your silence is for you not usually peaceful. It is a busy silence behind your fierce and faraway face. Sometimes I have desperately wanted to disturb it, to get your attention, to stamp my foot and insist that you *be here now.* What that usually meant was that I wanted you to pay more attention to me. I would tell you my troubles and wish you would comfort me and give me solace and understanding, but instead you would tell me what to do about my troubles and throw up your hands in dismay if I didn't do what you said. And then you would return to your silence. I came to learn that my needs and wishes and hopes were no match for it.

One time at night while flying out of Tan An (9th infantry division) we received an urgent mission. We picked the patient up without mishap. He had been shot high in the left chest area. The ground medic had done a good job in controlling the bleeding so all I could do was treat for shock, start an I.V. and tell the A.C. to haul ass to 3rd Field Hospital in Saigon.

The patient was a very large white male with a lot of meat on his arms; the kind that might be hard to hit even under ideal circumstances. I couldn't hit a vein. I tried and tried. And tried. I just couldn't hit him, even though I'd had mucho practice, mostly under far less than ideal conditions. About this time, I started seeing the lights of the city so I gave up on the I.V.

Then the guy quits breathing and goes into cardiac arrest. I never liked Ambu-bags so I whipped off my flight helmet and started mouth-to-mouth C.P.R. the old-fashioned way. I was not able to get his heart or breathing started but I did manage to cause him to vomit into my mouth. By this time, I had seen so much that even this didn't bother me very much. It did not make me sick or even turn my stomach. I merely spit out his puke, cleared an airway and continued mouth-to-mouth.

About this time, we landed at the dust-off pad across from 3rd Field and as always there was an ambulance waiting. The two medic/drivers saw me doing mouth-to-mouth. I told them I could ride along to continue.

They said no they could handle it. They also switched him rapidly from my litter to one of their own. I think they did this whenever possible as my litters were often rather messy; blood, mud, guts, etc. And after all, if their ambulance got dirty they might have to clean it!

As they sped recklessly away for their evening "mission" which consisted of driving from the dust-off pad to the ER at 3rd Field across the street, a distance of about ½ block, I noticed that both were seated in the front seats; neither attending the patient. I'm sure he was D.O.A.

We left, stopped for gas and went back to Tan An to await another mission. We walked into the bunker where the radio guy was and had a seat. Some of the crew would sleep in the chopper but I never did, at least until this night. I always thought it was madness to do so, a perfect stationary target for a satchel charge or R.P.G and loaded with JP-4—I always stuck by the radio guy, they always seemed to have one of the mostly secure bunkers, often beds and air conditioning, lawn chairs, etc. This one at Tan An had a small refrigerator which was always filled with beer & Coca-Cola. They always gave us some. No sooner than I sat down when the radio guy says to me, "So how is So & So?" I calmly said he's dead. The radio guy jumps out of his chair about four feet in the air, grabs the mic and starts talking (obviously to the Deceased's unit). Then he hangs up, looks at me with a look that could kill and says, "The medic says he was alive when he gave him to you!" I just kind of shook my head and shrugged my shoulders. He wouldn't even let me have a Coke. He was about 6'4" and looking at me like I was Ho Chi Minh or something. I opted to spend my first night ever in the ship. This guy scared me! Between laying on hundreds of gallons of JP-4, concern for R.P.G.'s and guilt over the D.O.A., I did not sleep. Perhaps if I had tried the I.V. one more time?? I guess I'll never know.

Whatever is buried in your silence is what causes you to check the perimeter of the property every single night at the river. It is what makes you resist my pleas not to bring all those guns into the house, what makes you persist in keeping the pistol by the side of the bed or in your pocket, what allows you over and over to ask me to admire the beauty of the artistry in the design of a rifle, what frustrates you in my revulsion and refusal to pick it up, to hold it, to see how it feels in the hand. Whatever is buried in your silence is what makes you rise out of sleep with your hands up and at the ready to defend yourself.

At those moments the look in your eyes speaks to me of the nature of your silence. It tells me that the phrase "post-traumatic stress disorder" is a travesty of failed perception and misuse of language. Yes, you certainly are living your life post-trauma. But that is the extent of the accuracy. Stress is something we take an aspirin for or a stretch break at work. Stress is the excuse for weekend getaways or blowing up when the restaurant meal comes cold. At worst, it causes an ulcer, which is relatively easily diagnosed and treated, or it causes a bad back, which is a little trickier but still only rarely requires traction or surgery. We build buildings and bridges to withstand stress during earthquakes, and we even respect stress for its capacity to keep us alert and engaged with our work. Better a job that causes us stress than one that bores us to death, we say. "Stress," it seems to me, describes what you suffer from about as accurately as "mistake" describes the Holocaust.

"Disorder" is about as inadequate. A disorder is a disturbance of order. Naming a condition a disorder implies assuming that orderliness is the norm, the preferred condition, and that the goal of treatment is a return to order. It carries with it somehow a suggestion that what we value is neatness, precision, even perhaps predictability. Now if those are the goals, it would indeed seem that what we want is to be fixed, settled, finished, left with no more questions or uncertainty. That is not my goal. That would be a ridiculous goal. It would be totally unrealistic, and I don't think you yearn for that any more than I do.

I don't know what is the right name for what you suffer. It has been described by others as moral pain or, more poetically, the dark night of the soul. I am not as interested in what to call it as I am in its effects. I think if our government had imposed on me what it imposed on you and then if I discovered that my growing list of physical illnesses were related to Agent Orange, I might likely go into a perpetual state of rage. [Agent Orange was the extremely toxic dioxin herbicide sprayed in Vietnam to defoliate the jungle and thus leave no cover for North Vietnamese soldiers. This substance was made by Monsanto and named for the orange canisters in which it was shipped. It turned out to cause serious, and in some cases deadly, health problems for the American soldiers coming in contact with it. These included open weeping sores on the skin, peripheral neuropathy, and various cancers.] That you are not in a perpetual rage is a marvel to me. Perhaps it is merely that the human body and mind are incapable of sustaining perpetual rage. In any case, it should come as no surprise to anyone that you do not respect authority, particularly government authority, that you have no patience with fools, that you would rather be alone in the woods than at work in an inefficient office that regularly screws up your paperwork and doesn't pay you what you deserve.

But there is more, isn't there? We are talking about more here than bureaucratic red tape and ignorant foolishness. We are even talking about more than extremely frightening physical illnesses, illnesses that may ultimately be deadly. We are talking about good and decent and fresh young men—no, a young man, you—being subjected by the government in a routine and businesslike fashion to unspeakable horror. It is an outrage then that the results should be passed off as a stress disorder. What your body and mind have done in response to the war is not a disorder. It is a totally normal response to that horror. In fact, I should think that not to respond as you have would indicate a disorder.

It is not surprising to me that you would want to anesthetize yourself and medicate yourself against pain. I would not want my nights lit up with flares showing my position to the Viet Cong while I was lowered ever so slowly from a chopper to the ground to pick up mangled and broken, or dead, bodies.

> A frequent unpleasant occurrence at night was landing on L/Z's marked by a strobe. We would be in radio contact with the folks on the ground, at the proper coordinates, but often there were 2 or 3 or even 4 strobes. We would have to pick one knowing that if it was the incorrect one it would be Charlie monitoring our radios, trying to lure us to his strobe so he could blow us away. This happened often.
> Another bad one at night that never went well for me was "land by the burning hooch." I only had a few of these, but every time we would take fire from more than one direction. This made each one get more and more scary.

If I thought every day of my life was borrowed time, who knows how I would choose to spend it?

> One night up at Nui Ba Den (the Black Virgin Mountain) I had a particularly bad experience. Not that going there was ever good:

Charlie held the slopes and surrounding area and it seemed that the weather was always treacherous for flying to the L/Z we controlled at the summit. It was very common to take massive fire both coming and going. This night the guy on the ground had both legs gone and the medic was freaking out. The weather was so nasty we could not see past the windshield. They filled numerous 55-gallon drums with kerosene or some other flammable liquid and lit them in an attempt to make an L/Z. We made dozens of "blind" approaches; all in vain. This went on for hours, so long in fact that we had to go somewhere to gas up.

When we got back, the folks on the ground were really freaking as they said if we could not get him out A.S.A.P. they would lose him. The weather was much worse. The four of us took a vote and it was unanimous that we would go for it. The A.C. said, "Hang on, we're going in and not pulling back this time, fuck it." We made our last blind approach and never did see the flames through the total blackout. We missed the peak altogether. By this time there was another dust-off on station and they made visual contact with us as we broke through the soup. They radioed urgently, "Dust-off so & so, you're going backwards & descending tail down." We were showing a forward air speed of 50 knots, but apparently we all had vertigo, and the head wind must have been a hundred.

The next thing I know we're nose straight up, tail down and dropping fast. The crew chief carried a tool box that weighed at least 100 pounds and it hit the ceiling. We were crashing backwards through trees, brush, and the cabin was filled with debris in the air like what shoots out of a lawn mower. I looked at the crew chief. He was without a doubt the calmest person in 4th Platoon and very well sun tanned. His face was as white as a sheet. I, myself, had never been so scared in my life! We were sliding backwards, down a cliff, chopping as we descended. I started to jump out as we must have been very close to the ground and I did not care for the idea of being burned alive. I hesitated for a split second, thinking that if I jumped, Charlie would have me as a P.O.W. Then we fell backwards off the edge of a cliff and the A.C. was able to regain control. All that I have just described of our last approach attempt occurred in five seconds or less.

While we circled above the soup trying to regain our composure, the other dust-off tried the same thing, got lucky and hit the L/Z. I think they all got Distinguished Flying Crosses; if not, they certainly deserved them.

But your story is not my story. It is not the story I have to tell. I want to tell you about a very surprising thing that happened to me this past fall. I was in a class in which we made what Jo Milgrom, the professor, called "handmade midrash." (Milgrom, 1992) We would make shapes out of found objects in response to some thematic question Jo Milgrom suggested, and only afterwards would we explore the theme verbally by interpreting what we had made with our hands. What we had made was itself the midrash, the interpretation of some sacred text.

Usually we made our midrash at home out of things we found there and brought it to class the following week. But one day, quite surprisingly, Jo Milgrom asked us to make a midrash on the spot. She had asked us to consider some part of the body that needed to be healed, the ill from which it suffered, and what we could do to bring about the healing. Having given that assignment, she dumped out on the table the motley contents of a shopping bag. We were to take what we wished and proceed in silence to make a midrash. We had about ten minutes to do it.

At first, I sat frozen. I had no idea what to do. In the past weeks, I had spent several days at home mulling over the assignments and letting my responses slowly form. In so doing, of course, I was partly defeating the purpose of handmade midrash. The idea was to make first and think afterwards. So, on this day Jo Milgrom was forcing me to honor the process that she knew to be profoundly meaningful.

But I, the introvert—worse yet, the introvert without a jot of talent for the visual arts—was stymied.

71

I used up several minutes just sitting there, numb. Finally, I galvanized myself into motion. I got up and moved toward the pile of stuff in the middle of the table, having no idea what I would pick or what I would do with it after I picked it. Mostly what was there looked to me like a welter of stuff, too various, too full of colors and shapes, so that all I could do was be confused by it all. Finally, I pulled out of the confusion one long torn strip of white cloth. That was all. I took it back to my chair and sat with it. While I was trying to figure out what to do, I started wrapping the strip of cloth around my left hand. I took off the ring that you had given me and put it on the table, and then I knew what I was doing, wrapping that hand.

When Jo gave the assignment—to think of a part of the body that needed healing—I immediately thought of your hands and the damage that Agent Orange has done to them. When she asked what the illness was, my silent response was the war. And as I wrapped that long bandage ever tighter around my left hand, I discovered I was crying, and in fact, I could not stop crying and I could not explain to anybody why I was crying. It was too complicated and too private and too horrible. It was that no matter what I did, there was nothing I could do that would heal you. I could only weep for my own powerlessness and your profound need for healing.

Finally, I did another surprising thing. I took the two ends of the cloth and tied them in a bow on top with my ring tied into the bow. I have always loved that ring, and I get many compliments on it for the interesting and asymmetrical design of the silver ingot.

I wear it on the finger where other women wear their wedding rings. When I took it off that day, it was difficult to remove, as a ring is that has been worn as many years as I have worn this one. I wondered what I was doing that day. Was I grieving that my ring was not a wedding ring? Was I acknowledging that our relationship was yet another casualty of war? These questions shook me badly. I did not tell you about any of this. But then, that was consistent with our silent dance, wasn't it? We have not talked of such things. We have not been able to.

Eventually I wriggled my hand out of its bandage, but I left the ring tied into the bedraggled bow for many days before I put it back on. I do not think I understood what was going on in me until I read Patience Mason's book. At one point she quotes somebody who says to the partner of a veteran that you can either commit yourself to staying and work through the problems that flow from that commitment or you can commit yourself to leaving and work through the problems that flow from that decision. But what causes the real pain and anxiety is not either of those commitments. It is the wavering of not being committed to either course of action. The time my ring stayed tied in the bow of bandage was wavering time.

I read something else this week about commitment. Steve Mason, a Vietnam veteran and poet (not as far as I know, related to Patience and Bob Mason), wrote of the "commitment worthy of a lifetime—to fight for peace in our hearts against the fierce enemies of our darkest natures." That says something perhaps about why I put the ring back on. The last words of Patience Mason's book are: "Recovery is not for sissies." We, you and I, are not sissies. Of that I am certain. We are both fighters and have been for a long time. And so, behold: It says here, here in this ring on my finger, I have signed on, enlisted, stepped forward. Here I am and I'm on for the long haul, wherever it leads.

Whatever does this mean? To begin with, it means I am going to have to speak up, start talking, break the silence, tell you how I'm feeling, and, as Patience says, try to paraphrase what I think you are saying, or not saying, and give you a chance either to confirm it or correct my misapprehensions. So –

I think it was a powerful act of courage for you to take part in the Winter Soldier encampment all those years ago and throw your medals in the heap. [In the spring of 1971, the VVAW investigated war crimes and atrocities, which was followed by five days of demonstration in Washington, D.C., to protest the war and lobby Congress. At the Washington encampment that April, a number of veterans, including Alan, pitched into a heap their Purple Hearts and other medals.]

I am very happy that you are becoming active in Veterans for Peace. It seems to me that you have the capacity to accomplish very important things there. This week I listened to a speaker who has worked with veterans from all our wars back as far as World War I. He said that some of the World War I veterans said that if the Civil War veterans had only told the truth to them about war when they were young, they would not have been willing to go to war themselves. The young need to hear from you about war. They need to hear the truth about it. I hope you will be able to tell them.

I think about the fact that my father was 18 when he went to fight in World War I. Forty years later when I wrote to him from a city on the Rhine, he wrote back that he had been in prison there. I remember that he could not stand the sound of fireworks on the Fourth of July. He could not even stand the sound of thunder. He always paced during storms. And he drank himself to sleep every night.

My brother went to World War II when he was 18. My brother is 16 years older than I am, and I remember a picture of me with him and a buddy he brought home once on leave. I was a little girl in a bonnet, and he and his buddy were proudly showing me their rifles. When my brother came home after the war, he spent a lot of time in the basement—working on an invention, he said, that would make a million dollars. My mother, who was his step-mother and who never could understand him, said that Richard always mumbled. He played his trumpet down there in the basement. And he drank.

My ex-husband's brother had just come back from Korea when I met him. He never talked much, and one summer he stopped talking altogether for months. He sat on the swing in the back yard or in the rocking chair, and he stared. And he drank.

And now I think of you. What you and all those others before you, and all those who died, have done for the rest of us is to change us, to show up the triviality in our lives for what it is. You give us the opportunity to stand with you shoulder to shoulder in this work of healing from war.

What shall we do next? Some people talk about the importance of remembering. They spell it remembering. They speak of the capacity of time plus memory to transform the past, to make what has not been whole, whole. Maya Lin described the Washington Vietnam Memorial that she designed as "cutting the earth open with a knife and letting grass grow over it to heal the wounds." Well, I know that when you and I visited the wall, we did not react to it as strongly as others apparently do. Or at least we did not say we did. But I know it took my breath away when I went back to Kent and saw the hill all the way up from the Commons to Taylor Hall covered with blooming daffodils, one for every American who died in Vietnam.

Some veterans have gone back to Vietnam. I wonder if you have ever thought of doing that. I wonder what that would be like for you and what you would do there.

I know I rejoiced to hear of the healing that happens in the Vet Center groups, and I know it is up to you whether you check out the centers in Jacksonville and Orlando. I cannot get you to go to one of them any more than I can get you to put the guns away or stop drinking or put your arms around me or tell me that you love me. I can only tell you what I need.

Ever since I helped build a house long ago, I have loved the sounds and smells and the feel of construction —the smell of fresh sawn cedar and the sound of long roofing nails being driven home, the banter and working together and holding up your end and struggling together against the elements and for the solid beauty of the work. Even more than building, I have a passion for rebuilding, reconstruction, making whole again what has been broken, burned, ravaged. It is sometimes risky business. There are hazards. And the result will never be the same as the original. It may not even much resemble it. That's all right with me. After you read this past fall what I wrote about my "vocational aspirations," you asked me if there was a place for you in the community I envision. The answer is yes. It is a community engaged in reconstruction. I believe it has the power to bring meaning where there was none and to transform what has been unbearable into new understanding and commitment to justice and human dignity. As Patience Mason says, this work is not for sissies. It is for me though, and for you too, I hope . . .

With love,
Barbara

Chapter 3

Dying in Florida

Being together is knowing
even if what we know
is that we cannot really be together
caught in the teeth of the machinery
of the wrong moments of our lives.

—Marge Piercy, from "Bridging"

As we had said we would, Alan and I continued to conduct our long-distance relationship mostly by telephone. Email had not made its way into our world, and he was not much for writing letters. However, I came to know well what the quality of his voice revealed about how far gone he was into his nightly stupor. There were more and more nights when all I could do was say we would talk again soon and then hang up. I did know that he would read, sometimes over and over, anything I wrote to him. So, if there was something I especially wanted him to take in, I would not try to address it on the phone. I would send him a letter.

I spent most of the following July with Alan at the Florida cottage. Shortly after I got back to school, I wrote him this letter.

***

August 5, 1994
Berkeley, California

Dear Alan,

I am troubled about a couple of things, and I decided I would try to give words to them on paper instead of bringing them up on the phone. I am not looking for any answer from you so much as I am hoping that you will think about these things. I know you have always taken seriously what I have written to you, and I have always appreciated that.

I am troubled about how big a role firearms have in your life—and how dangerous is the potential for accident. I know you always wanted a pistol by the bed at night. But it seems now that the number of weapons has grown enormously, and that you are devoting an enormous amount of attention to them. I saw a lot of ammunition in the cottage, and I noticed how much time you spent reading gun magazines. I wondered about the human-shaped targets you have. I gather you engage in target practice from the dock, which is how the top railing got damaged. I am not sure. Maybe you were shooting a poisonous snake, which is quite okay to do. But I worry that you are shooting there for sport. I am unhappy if that is so, that just because I'm not there, you feel it is okay not to honor my wish not to have shooting happen there.

What has caused my concern to become grave is the accident you described to me in which a gun went off in the house, plus the fact that you were wearing a loaded gun outside of a holster routinely in your pocket or tucked into your belt or your brace. I can still see one moment when you were very drunk, having trouble keeping your balance, and the pistol was there in your very loose belt.

I don't know how else to say it—it seems to me that you are in grave danger of accidentally killing somebody else, or yourself, as a result of having unholstered loaded guns in the cottage, especially on your person, most especially when you are drunk. I know you were pleased about the fact that you were drunk only twice in the 25 days I was there. I was pleased by those 23 days too. But one minute with a loaded gun when you are out of control because of either alcohol or drugs or both is one minute too many.

I am so happy that you are getting treatment for PTSD that I hardly know what to do, and also that you are taking action to get to the hospital. There is much to be hopeful about now.

I know I told you when I was there that I couldn't prevent you from combining alcohol and guns and that I was not going to subject myself to that danger. So, you have already heard it, and I thought all this week about not writing this letter. But I still need to—because it's not just about protecting myself from that danger. I'm here, not there.

What I want you to know—one more time—is that I love you, and I don't want you to die. I want you to get better, and I'm excited to have you really taking action to "beat it," as you say. So, you just have to hear me, please hear me, when I say you are in no shape to manage a gun when you've been drinking.

Lately, I have heard you insist you were not drunk when you clearly were. And you know it doesn't matter whether it's drugs or alcohol. It's the result that matters. The point is, you are not a good judge of how drunk you are.

Therefore, I would conclude that an unholstered loaded gun is a menace at any time.

Now, I know that after all that, if you've made it this far, you probably feel like this is enough—but I also need to say a little bit about that picture you wanted me to look at and that I did look at. I don't know, of course, but I suspect that picture has become for you the symbol of everything horrible about the war and yourself. I can't know but I can guess at why you were very insistent that I look at it, and yet you said you weren't ready to talk about it. That was your response in the daytime when I asked you if you wanted to talk about it, and I respected your wish and so didn't ask any more questions.

The night before though, when you were very drunk, you did say a little about it. That's when you got very upset and eventually called the crisis line. The reason I'm going over all this is that it has to do with my concern over the fact that you kept that picture out on your desk where you would see it every time you sat down to make a phone call or write something.

I have the impression that having that picture there, where you have to see it all the time, is torture for you. It seems to me, in other words, that you are torturing yourself with it. That picture, when you are drunk, produces a misery that you aren't then in a position to be able to handle.

I guess all I can do is suggest that there isn't any requirement that you be tortured in order to heal. You could put the picture away in a safe place where you could find it and bring it out when you are ready to deal with it in therapy. I would just like to suggest that you consider doing that.

I am aware that I may have made some assumptions here that aren't true. You don't owe me any explanations or answers, as I said before. I just have to let you know what's on my mind and ask you please to think about these things.

Love,
Barbara

***

The picture that I wrote about in this letter was of two young Vietnamese boys. They were lying on the ground, dead. Alan never did tell me the story of the picture, why he had it or what it represented to him and why it had such a profoundly terrible effect on him. He never would say either why he was so insistent that the picture remain in its prominent place on his desk where he would have to see it constantly.

But I don't believe he needed to tell me the answers to any of my questions about the picture for me to know the answers. As surely as I know anything at all, I know that Alan killed those boys, or at least he was in his own mind responsible for their death. It really doesn't matter exactly how they died. For him, looking at those dead boys was the perpetual punishment he thought he had to endure to atone for that crime. Likewise, that one killing no doubt came for him to represent every death in Viet Nam for which he thought he was in any way responsible. Alan was 20 years old when he came back from Viet Nam. No sinner in any circle of Dante's Inferno was made to suffer worse torment than Alan Morris suffered every day of the quarter-century he lived as a veteran of that war.

Another unpleasant night mission I vividly recall was also an urgent one out of Tan An. It was over by a special forces camp, I believe, Much Hoe, over by Cambodia. It was a major battle with gun fire, rockets, etc., everything you can name going off everywhere. I couldn't believe we were even thinking of going in but we circled the area while jets & Cobras pounded the area. I think Puff was there also.

There were many, many urgent casualties so we headed in to what was the closest thing they had to an L/Z. We approached with a Cobra on each side of us with everything they had blazing away. I had Rolling Stones music cranked up in my head set and the rockets and tracers were actually in beat with the music. I was amazed, it was like some professional rock concert light show. To this day when I hear certain Stones songs I get goose bumps and the hair on my arms stands up.

The L/Z was water about waist deep with old stumps sticking up everywhere so we could only hover several feet in the air. I no sooner started to pull up the first wounded Green Beret when the A.R.V.N's swarmed us; some wounded & some not. In an instant the ship was totally overloaded & people were climbing on each other, the skids, the edge of the floor, anything they could get their hands on including me. It was like being swarmed by ants. We couldn't pull pitch, started bouncing around and spinning. It was like being chained to the ground, the chains being made of human links. It now became us or them. I grabbed a sturdy pole used to support litters with both my hands to keep from being pulled off the ship. We were taking fire from 3 directions and everything you can name was going off, mostly right by us. I started kicking people in the face, chest, wherever, to knock them off the ship so we wouldn't crash. I stomped their fingers as they tried to hang on. Somehow, we managed to take off. We must have had 2 or 3 times the maximum load you are supposed to be able to fly with. As I looked back and down at the L/Z it was just like a 4th of July fireworks display. I was so cramped in I couldn't move but it didn't matter anyway as I was so scared I was frozen numb for at least 5 minutes. I think I was in some form of shock. As usual, we somehow managed to make it back.

A couple of months after I wrote that letter to Alan, I wrote another one to accompany his "stressor letter" to the VA, substantiating his claim for benefits incurred on account of PTSD. The instructions say that a stressor letter is supposed to describe in detail the trauma or traumas in the course of military service that produced post-traumatic stress, and also to describe in detail the post-traumatic symptoms of the stress. Alan was evidently afraid his own account would not be persuasive enough. He asked me to substantiate it, and I agreed.

**

September 21, 1994
Berkeley, California

To Whom It May Concern:

My intimate relationship with Alan Morris began eight years ago this month. I would like to be able to say that we have been partners; however, he has let me know that he does not regard us that way. He says we are friends. Every time I have tried to get him to express how he feels about me or what our relationship means to him, all he does is repeat that he does not have feelings. Never once has he ever said to me, "I love you." Nevertheless, I have cared deeply for him, and we have shared our lives with each other over the past eight years.

In many respects they have not been easy years. Alan has a very serious drinking problem. He often starts drinking before noon, and although sometimes he seems to be able to drink quite a lot without appearing drunk, he often is quite drunk by supper time. When he is drunk, he loses interest in eating. He also gets agitated, cannot sit still, finds excuses to go for a ride, becomes loud and belligerent, and seriously overreacts to anything he regards as ill treatment by others. He regularly drives drunk, either not understanding or refusing to acknowledge how seriously impaired he is and how dangerous to others and himself on the highway.

For the past year he has had an array of prescribed medications, which he has been taking in what I presume to be doses much larger than prescribed. His speech becomes badly slurred. On the telephone he is quick to tell me that he is not drunk. I can in fact tell the difference between the effects of alcohol and the effects of pills on his speech. However, I believe he is abusing drugs and alcohol together, so much so that I live in fear of his accidental death.

Sometimes when he is drunk, he just sits and stares—although he does that a great deal when he is not drunk too. Sometimes when he is drunk, he gets very excited and hyperactive. He may go for a boat ride and weave the boat dangerously back and forth. He wants to shoot guns then, and he actually whoops. It is very strange because such times seem to be the only ones when he is really enjoying himself and when he comes close to being demonstrative with me. However, there is no pleasure in it for me. He seems quite wild then and all I want to do is get away from him because I fear an accident.

Ever since Alan and I got together, he has insisted on having a loaded pistol by the bed every night. This has always been a matter of grave concern to me because of his nightmares. I always had some fear that if I got up in the night to go to the bathroom, he might mistake me for an intruder and shoot me. Also, I have had to exercise great caution in getting into bed if he was asleep before I got there. Anytime he is awakened, he sits up with a start with his arms raised in front of him ready to defend himself. Before he would go to bed, he would always take a walk around the house outside. "Checking the perimeter," he called it. Away from home, he is always more or less nervous. Whenever we would go to a restaurant, he would want to sit with his back to the wall. Also, he has a habit, of which I think he is generally unaware, of sitting with his legs crossed and violently swinging his top (usually right) leg back and forth. Whenever anyone says or does anything that upsets him in the slightest, his right leg starts swinging. Sometimes it twitches violently in his sleep.

I moved to California in August of 1993 to go back to school. We spent a week together in January, and I spent the month of July with him in Florida. During this past year, he has been having therapy at the VA for

PTSD. I am extremely glad he is getting therapy. However, by July it was evident that the therapy was bringing his memories of Vietnam to the surface with dramatic effects. A few times in the past he had shown me some pictures taken in Vietnam, and he had been able to talk about it a little bit with me after we went to see some Vietnam movies, "Platoon," in particular. But "Apocalypse Now" seems to be the movie that has the greatest effect on him. While I was in Florida in July, there was a program on TV about the making of "Apocalypse Now." We watched it, and after that he had the worst night I have ever seen him have.

It seems now that the only people he really has any interest in being around are other Vietnam veterans. This is understandable to me, yet I fear that it is not healthy. Alan has taken to wearing fatigues again all the time. The house is now full of weapons and ammunition. He was going around with an unholstered pistol either stuck in the front of his belt or in his back pocket. When he told me that the splintered wood in the ceiling was the result of a pistol having fallen off a chair one night and discharged, I refused to spend another minute in the house with him without all the pistols being holstered.

He also was quite insistent that I look at a picture from Vietnam that turned out to be a picture of some dead people. He left the picture out on his desk where he had to look at it every time he sat down to work or use the telephone. That picture seemed to evoke for him all the horror of Vietnam, and it seemed to me that he was punishing himself by forcing himself to look at it constantly. Looking at it agitated him terribly when he

The cypress swamp and woods across the river from the house.

was drunk, so much so that one night he called the VA Crisis Line in the middle of the night while I was there. When he talked about the picture, he referred to himself as a "condemned man." He is always worse at night and always worse when he is drunk. He stays up far into the night staring at the TV set. He wants the TV on all the time when he is in the house, no matter whether there is anything good on or not. He tells me that sometimes in the middle of the night when he cannot sleep, he takes a rifle and rows across the river to the woods across from the house. Then he says he just sits there in the woods with his rifle for hours.

Alan quit his job last June because all the driving it required was causing him impossible back pain. Now he is living on his Unemployment benefits and his 401-K money and trying to get his mother's house in Ohio sold so that he will have enough money to support her while he goes into the hospital for four months of treatment for PTSD, including a month of detoxification. I am extremely glad that he has recognized the seriousness of his condition and is taking steps to get it treated. At the same time, I fear for him. Being out of work, he doesn't have the controls that a job produces. There is nothing to prevent his reliving Vietnam more and more, and the reliving appears to be more and more dangerous.

When I got back to California after my month in Florida, I wrote Alan a letter about my concerns about his carrying an unholstered pistol while drunk, and about his fixation on the picture of the dead people. I told him that I have decided I cannot sleep in the same house with him until he has had his period of hospitalization. I know there are no guarantees about the success of the hospitalization, but I am hopeful about it because he continues to say that he is "going to beat this." Meanwhile, I am not willing to place myself in what I now regard as real physical danger. Alan has never been violent with me at all, and I have not feared and do not fear intentional violence from him. What I fear is an accident. I am not willing to risk it under the present circumstances. I still care for him as much as I ever have, and I very much want to see him get better.

Sincerely,
Barbara Child

***

One day we picked up a load of wounded Vietnamese civilians. Most I easily dealt with except for one old man. I had him on a litter on the floor by the transmission. He had a stomach wound, left leg gone about mid-thigh and a multiple compound fracture of the right arm. Treating the stomach wound was easy, and I had no trouble with the traumatic amputation. However, I could not handle his right arm. He kept flipping it back and forth, dragging it along the protective covering that covered the transmission housing. Its motion was in beat with the whompf-whompf of the rotors. It was hypnotic.

Between not knowing how to handle the situation and the bizarre flipping of his right arm, I was paralyzed. I just stared at the mangled arm, flipping back and forth.

Recently I had an incident occur about this arm. I certainly must have been dreaming, but I saw this arm crawling and flipping toward me from under my dresser as I slept. I was just about to shoot the arm when I woke up.

When I awoke I was seated upright in bed and my .38 from under my pillow was cocked and ready to shoot the arm. I almost shot a round into a hard, concrete floor.

Alan and I both went to Kent for the 25th anniversary commemoration of the killings, May 4, 1995. He flew from Florida and I flew from Berkeley. I stayed with my oldest and dearest friends in Kent, Anne Reid and Bob Howard, whom I have known since the 1960s. Alan stayed with friends as well, though I'm not sure with whom. Possibly Ruth Gibson, who was his girlfriend in

Kent in the early 1970s and with whom he maintained a friendship over the years. There is a picture on my dresser of Alan and me in the crowd on the Commons on May 4, 1995. It is the last picture that was ever taken of us together. We are standing up. Seated around us are Anne and Bob and the other friends with whom I was sitting for the commemo-

On the Kent State University Commons, May 4, 1995, at the 25th anniversary commemoration of the killings.

ration ceremonies. I'm quite sure Alan had not been sitting there with us. He was probably sitting with Ruth Gibson. In any case, what I do remember is that Ruth took the picture. Our faces tell the tale. My face, indeed my whole body, is strained, and I am looking somewhere off into the distance. Alan, looking simply sad, has his hand on my shoulder. He is smiling slightly and looking at the face behind the camera.

***

The following school year was my last at Starr King. By that time, I was no longer fantasizing about ministering to homeless veterans in the North Florida woods, but I had a new idea that very much appealed to me. The married couple who served jointly as Florida District Executives for the Unitarian Universalist Association were getting ready to retire. I had watched them in action over the years, I liked what I saw of what they did, and I very much wanted to succeed them. I had been serving on the Florida District's Conflict Management Team. I had been an administrator in law schools for a number of years, and before that I had served as student ombudsman when I was on the faculty in the Kent State University English Department. In short, I had loads of experience managing conflict and otherwise navigating the dynamics of people in groups.

I got my heart set on the Florida District Executive's position. In addition to everything else appealing about it, it would mean I could live wherever I chose in Florida. I probably wouldn't want to live full time at the cottage on the Santa Fe River, but this job would give me the flexibility to allow Alan and me to make some progress at last on our relationship as well as his healing. And to make this picture even brighter, I was lucky enough to be able to arrange to have the final six months of my schooling be an internship with a minister I very much admired, Rev. Marni Harmony, at the First Unitarian Church of Orlando.

Amy Jo Smith, a dear friend from Gainesville, came to help me move out of my studio apartment in Berkeley and to share in driving the rental truck to Florida. I had let Alan know that while I would get a studio apartment for January to June in Orlando, I was going to move most of my belongings into the cottage on the Santa Fe. I would come up there often on days off so we could see each other a lot. But before I arrived, I needed him to move himself and his things out of the cottage. By then he had moved his mother up from Ponce Inlet and got her a little house nearby in Three Rivers Estates. He could live there with her.

By the time I got to Florida that winter, Alan had indeed managed to move most of his things out of the cottage. I remember spending New Year's Eve watching TV with him at the house he now shared with his mother. I remember noticing when the axe flew out of his hand when he tried to chop some firewood. He simply couldn't control it. Soon after that, he could no longer control a can opener. And he had taken to walking with a stick. When I was at the cottage and he came over there, he took to knocking on the door. I winced. He didn't need to knock, I said. But he kept on doing it every time he came over. And eventually, I gave up trying to talk him out of it.

Years before, when we first got together in Gainesville, he had said he was never going to live as an invalid. In those days, he said that when the time came, he would take a boat out on the ocean and just not come back. But that would be far, far in the future. That was not something to contemplate anytime soon. By the winter and spring of 1996, that old plan had managed to get buried somewhere in my head where I couldn't reach it. Besides, the Santa Fe River was pretty far inland, nowhere near the ocean, and the rowboat at the dock, even with the ten-speed motor attached, wouldn't be going any further than maybe upriver to Pope's Store.

Anyhow, such talk was no longer relevant. Alan was getting at least some kind of treatment from the VA. And there was a plan for him to go into the hospital for detox and intensive treatment for his PTSD. He had written his stressor letter and sent it in, and I had written my "To Whom It May Concern" letter to go along with it. Surely, he would begin receiving financial compensation soon from the VA for his PTSD. I was doing my internship with a wonderful minister whom I deeply admired, and doing it in Orlando, close enough that I could come up to the cottage and we could see each other often. And best of all, the Florida District Executive's position was coming open, I had applied, and I was so well qualified that, surely, I would get the job.

That was my assessment of things as 1996 got underway. My internship progressed beautifully over the spring. It was determined that the Orlando congregation would ordain me, with major participation from my home congregation, the Unitarian Universalist Fellowship of Gainesville. The date was set for the ordination —June 2, just a couple of weeks after Starr King's graduation ceremonies, which would happen in Berkeley on May 17. There were so many things to look forward to, and my attention stayed on them. After all, they took planning and preparation, at least partly by me.

The tradition at Starr King School graduation ceremonies is that each graduate speaks briefly, and graduates take these speeches very seriously, preparing their remarks thoughtfully. These are no off-the-cuff presentations. Nobody wings it. I remember how seriously I took the task of preparing what I would say. I wrote my graduation speech on the porch at the cottage on the

Santa Fe, which seemed particularly appropriate since it was on that porch, overlooking the river, where I had written all those essays that became part of my application to Starr King School.

Alan wasn't going with me to Berkeley. I don't remember why not. My friend Amy Jo Smith from Gainesville was going with me. The graduation ceremonies would be on Friday evening, and Amy

Speaking at Starr King School graduation ceremony, May 17, 1996.

Jo and I looked forward to spending the rest of the weekend doing whatever we pleased in Berkeley. The day before she and I flew to California, I sat on the porch at the cottage rehearsing my speech. Alan stopped by on his way to taking his mother for a doctor's appointment. He didn't sit down, just stuck his head out the door from the living room to the porch and wished me a great weekend. He was in a hurry, running late. I don't think he stopped long enough to say good-bye.

Given the three-hour time difference between Florida and California, as best I can figure, Alan shot himself to death at just about the same time I was delivering my graduation speech.

Chapter 4

Mementos, Memorials, and a Ritual of Grieving

They shouldn't call it suicide,
this self-inflicted gunshot wound—
the trigger squeezed so many years ago—
day by day, the fragment slipped inside.
His name won't be chiseled on the Wall.
He won't reflect your face for you.
He doesn't qualify. He missed
the cut-off date. He died too late.

—H. Palmer Hall
from "The Fortunate Son"
For Lewis Puller; d. 1994, from a festering wound

Most of my friends said it was a terrible thing Alan did to me, casting a pall forever over my memories of my graduation. But I have never thought of it that way. I have always thought he did me an enormous favor, doing it when I was not there. I remember a vet buddy of his in Gainesville who shot himself in bed one night watching television with his wife at his side. I have always been grateful to Alan that he did no such thing as that.

And I have been grateful to my Gainesville friends for choosing not to call me in Berkeley but letting me enjoy my weekend celebration untarnished. When I returned that Sunday night to my tiny apartment in Orlando, there was a message on my answering machine from my friend Suzanne Autumn, asking me to call her. She did not sound good. Oh dear, I thought, something is not going well in Suzanne's life. I decided to wait until the next morning to return her call. I was just too tired that night after my long weekend.

And so it was that I learned of Alan's death while I was at the Orlando church where my beloved internship supervisor, Marni Harmony, came running to minister to me. I will always be grateful to her and also to Suzanne, for carrying the burden of my grief that whole weekend by not calling me in California.

I also discovered later what a gift the Gainesville Veterans for Peace gave me. Alan shot himself in the cottage, and the Sheriff's Department apparently did not do a very good job of cleaning up. The Vets for Peace went out there and did what needed to be done. Still, it was enormously hard for me to go back into the cottage and to spend the night there. My friend Amy Jo went along the first time I went back there. Amy Jo has always been there when I needed her.

When we arrived at the cottage, remnants of the yellow "Police Line, Do Not Cross" tape still clung to the door frame. For a moment, I had the crazy thought that I was not allowed to go in. I did know better, of course, and in we went. And it didn't take very long for me to be able to stay there by myself.

I became obsessed with discovering where, exactly, Alan had been when he fired that Colt .45. I'd had some brief conversation with someone from the criminal investigation unit at the Sheriff's Department about some detail or other, but that person had not been very forthcoming, and I had no wish for further conversation. Maybe I didn't want those officials to think I was morbid. Maybe I didn't think it was any of their business what I wanted to know. I'm not sure. Anyhow, I decided this was an investigation for me to do on my own. In a way that I could not explain, this was between Alan and me. No one else was to be involved.

When Alan was living at the cottage and I was in Berkeley, he had his big desk in front of the window that looked directly out to the river. When I moved my few things back from Berkeley and he moved his things out, I put in front of the window the little round white pedestal table and two chairs that had been in my kitchen everywhere I had lived for the previous twenty years. I bought them for the kitchen in my first house, in Brady Lake, Ohio, just outside of Kent. I loved that table and chairs. They had served me well.

As I prepared to do my investigation that day, I sat down at the little white table to think.Leaning against the wall a few feet away were the disassembled pieces of the black particle board desk I had bought for my studio apartment in Berkeley. The pieces were leaning there waiting to be reassembled or else disposed of, since I had no more need of that cheap desk. I sat there at the white table, staring at the black desk, trying to think.

And then I saw the round hole, straight ahead of me at eye level in the black desk. I went over there and pulled the desk boards away from the wall. Sure enough, there was an indentation in the cement block wall behind the desk where the bullet had finally stopped. The mystery was solved. Alan had been sitting at the little white table looking out at the river when he pulled the trigger. For some reason that I could not quite explain, being certain of that made me glad. It made me glad to think that the beautiful river he loved so much was the last thing he ever saw.

I put the white table and chairs and the black desk out by the mailbox at the edge of the road with the sign: FREE. In my mind's eye, I can still see the legs of a white chair sticking out of the open trunk of somebody's car as it pulled away.

Soon enough, condolence notes began to arrive, most of them from friends of mine, people who had not known Alan. But Alan's mother put into my hands an envelope that contained the Spanish coin called a "piece of eight" that Alan had worn around his neck. I had a companion coin, a smaller one, that he had given me. The two coins now sit in a small jewelry box of their own on my dresser. When Enid gave me the piece of eight, there was no card with it. But she had written in her shaky script on the envelope:

> Would like you to have Alan's "Piece of Eight" or Doubloon. Hope you are never short of money, but if so, or the church, it is worth something. Sorry I didn't have any silver polish. The coin is from the [ship called] Conception.
>
> Love & peace
> Enid XO

And it meant a lot to me to receive a note from Ruth Gibson:

> Dear Barbara,
>
> My heart goes out to you at this dreadful time. Alan loved you and truly valued your friendship. You must be feeling shock and great pain. I am feeling those things now and want to reach out to you and Enid in support. Although we grieve, we know Alan is with God and take comfort in that certainty.
>
> Love,
> Ruth

Another card came in the mail that I did not expect to receive. Gloria Emerson had been a war correspondent for *The New York Times* in Vietnam. Her book *Winners and Losers* (Emerson, 1976) is some of the most powerful writing I ever read about that war. Back in my Kent State teaching days, I used to offer an Emerson essay called "Getting Back" (Emerson, 1974) as one of my primary examples of eloquent dissent.

At some point while I was in Berkeley, the Gainesville Vets for Peace brought Gloria Emerson to Florida. She met Alan, and they talked about writing something together about the war. When I learned of it later, this seemed to me an extraordinary honor conferred on Alan by both the Vets for Peace and Gloria Emerson herself. I remember how pleased I was for Alan that such a collaboration might happen. Someone from Vets for Peace let her know of Alan's death, and I decided to write to her as well. She wrote back:

Dear Barbara,

I was deeply moved by your letter and thank you for writing during a time of such turmoil and pain of your own. ... I was horribly shaken [by Alan's death.] ... I think he was deathly tired of the struggle, and neither love nor money could have saved him. But I feel such sorrow at the waste of his gifts. He spoke of you, of course, such a deep part of his life.

Gloria Emerson

***

My minister at the Unitarian Universalist Fellowship of Gainesville, Rev. Jack Donovan, helped me put together a memorial service for Alan. I read parts of my "Open Letter to a Vietnam Veteran" as a eulogy. I brought into the sanctuary the Kent VVAW banner, which had been hanging on the wall at the cottage for years. At the end of the service, I gave it to the leaders of the Gainesville Vets for Peace, who attended the service in full force.

Someone else also arrived at that service whom I did not expect to see there and whom I did not want to see. This was the man who had sold Alan the Colt .45 just a week or so before. I don't remember how I knew he was the seller. Maybe he introduced himself to me that day and told me. Maybe he was sorry he had sold Alan that revolver. Maybe he was sorry Alan had killed himself with it. Anyway, I tolerated his presence at the memorial service until the time when we invited people to share their memories and reflections. This man got up to speak. I have in my mind's eye this image of myself preventing him from doing so. I see myself rising up out of my chair in the front row next to Jack Donovan, telling this man he was not invited to speak, and then taking him by the elbow and leading him right out of the church. I probably in fact did none of those things. I probably only wish I had.

While I was in seminary taking Jo Milgrom's class on "Handmade Midrash," I had been struck by images she shared of the grief ritual of rending one's garments, or the garments of the beloved who has died. In her book, she explains the biblical background, the paradigm provided by the exile from Eden. "Confronted with ... loss, biblical persons tore their garments." (Milgrom, 1992) The Hebrew word for tearing is "kriah." It means "to call out." In class, Jo Milgrom mentioned the value of calling out what one is being separated from. She demonstrated by tearing a piece of muslin slowly, "pausing every several inches to hear the tearing and to call out—or cry out—a sigh, a word, a feeling..." She instructs in her book: "Tear, call out, read, write— altering the order to your own needs, again and again, until you feel you can stop. When the *kriah* is done, the rebuilding can begin." (Milgrom, 1992)

After the memorial service, I went out to the cottage and built a bonfire in the yard. I tore to shreds everything of Alan's that I could tear and broke everything I could break. And then I took it all outside and threw it on the fire. I don't remember whether I called out while I was at it. I do remember that it took a long time for everything to burn.

The Gainesville memorial service was on May 27. Six days later, on June 2, I was ordained as a minister at the First Unitarian Church of Orlando. This celebration had been planned for a long time, with the Gainesville congregation taking significant part. A talented fabric artist in the Gainesville congregation, Norma Zabel, had made me a clerical stole, which she was going to present to me at my ordination as a gift of the Gainesville congregation. It had on it some of my favorite symbols—the Unitarian Universalist Service Committee's flaming chalice, symbol of work for justice and against oppression; the ankh, ancient Egyptian symbol of male and female, symbol of the constant regeneration of the world; the spiral, symbol of constant movement from without to within and from within to without; a triangle, replicated over and over inside itself in a rainbow of colors, at once representing diversity and the three stages of life; the Fool from the first Tarot card, jumping over the side of a cliff to smell a flower, which a friend said reminded her of me when I left the law school for the seminary; and finally a river, to represent the Santa Fe in North Florida, which I had always thought of as "my river"—well, Alan's and my river, place of refuge and solitude, but also source of constant motion and change.

The order of service for my ordination had been printed. Invitations had gone out. Speakers had prepared their parts. There was no way that ordination was not going to happen that Friday evening at the Orlando church. The previous Sunday in her pastoral prayer, Marni Harmony mentioned the death "out of season" of Barbara Child's partner Alan Morris. Marni is as wise a minister as any I know. What she did with that prayer was to eliminate any need for me to pretend at my ordination that things were other than they were. What she also did was give me what I needed to take up my part. All those people had prepared a magnificent celebration. They deserved to have me fully present and fully engaged in the spirit of my ordination. And so I was.

It is often the lot of a minister on a given day to officiate at a wedding in the morning and a memorial service in the afternoon, or vice versa. And it is essential to be fully present and engaged in both. How fortunate I was to have a practice session with not a matter of hours but six whole days between two such enormously important rites of passage.

The memorial service at the Unitarian Universalist Fellowship of Gainesville was the first of several celebrations of Alan's life. On July 6, Alan's old Kent friends who were still in the area held a memorial gathering at Kent State University. I sent Ruth Gibson excerpts from my "Open Letter to a Vietnam Veteran," which she included in the program. Afterward, she sent me a copy of the program, which included a picture of Alan surely taken the year before on the 25th anniversary of the May 4 killings. In this picture, Alan was wearing the tee shirt with the picture of the dust-off helicopter on it that he wore in the picture Ruth took of him and me on the Commons that day. Only this copy of the picture was oval shaped and had "In Memoriam" written around the rim.

One of the speakers at the Kent gathering was Tom Grace, who a quarter of a century before had a bullet shot through his left foot by a member of the Ohio National Guard. (Grace, 2016) Years later he let me know that he had invited Alan's mother to send some of Alan's personal effects, including commendations from his Vietnam service, to the Kent State Special Collections. And thus it was that one day over two decades after Alan's death, I sat down at a table in the Special Collections and went through what was labeled the "Morris Collection." I found in that big box, in addition to the original framed "In Memorium" picture, many framed commendations, many ribbons, a shiny green pin in the shape of a helicopter with the word "Dust-off" at the bottom, and to my surprise, Alan's Purple Heart. It was true then, as I only half remembered Alan's telling me, the pitching out of medals at the Winter Soldier Encampment in Washington had been a political gesture; after it was all over, the soldiers got their medals back.

The week following the memorial gathering at Kent State, on July 12, Bill Hutchinson, one of the Gainesville Vets for Peace and a fine musician, put on a "Musical Remembrance" in his music venue in nearby High Springs, Florida, that he called The Theatre of Memory. Finally, that year's 10th Annual Winter Soldier Peace Concert put on by the Gainesville Vets for Peace on December 26 was dedicated to Alan's memory. The program included the quotation I had put on the back of the order of service for the Gainesville Fellowship service, the words of a 19th century author otherwise unknown to me:

> It is not that we are singled out for a special judgment; when we give up our dead, we but enter into a common sorrow, a sorrow that visits the proudest and humblest, that has entered into unnumbered hearts before us and will enter into innumerable ones after us, a sorrow that should make the world one, and dissolve all other feelings into sympathy and love.—W.M. Salter

Part Two

I Will Wait for You

Chapter 5

Alan Will Be Coming Soon

It may be that when we no longer know what to do,
we have come to our real work,
and that when we no longer know which way to go,
we have come to our real journey.
The mind that is not baffled is not employed.
The impeded stream is the one that sings.

—"The Real Work," by Wendell Berry

It wasn't the first time I had signed up for a public program at Pacifica Graduate Institute outside of Santa Barbara, California. In fact, I had first discovered Pacifica some twenty years before, in 1996, when quite by accident I came across a brochure for a Pacifica program that listed as one of the speakers someone named Dennis Patrick Slattery. I couldn't resist going to the program if for no other reason than to find out whether this was the same Dennis Patrick Slattery who had been one of my best students in the Kent State University English Department in the mid-1960s. It was. By then he was on the core faculty at Pacifica, and I was serving in my first ministry at the Sepulveda Unitarian Universalist Society in the San Fernando Valley of Los Angeles. I had returned to California that summer of 1996 after I was turned down for the position of Florida District Executive.

When I went to that Pacifica program, I was delighted to discover what had become of Dennis Slattery, and I was taken by Pacifica's array of public programs in addition to its advanced degree programs in depth psychology and mythology. I began attending a weekend public program every so often, even after my ministry took me to other parts of the country. A weekend in Santa Barbara was always a treat. I could see old friends there and the Pacific Ocean, itself an old friend.

When the 2015 Pacifica Public Programs catalog arrived, I found myself drawn to a program that wasn't going to be for just one weekend. Instead it would be an intensive spread out over four weekends from late February through late May. It certainly wasn't the title that drew me in. The title was too long, and it contained everything but the kitchen sink: "Alchemy, Romanticism, *The Red Book*, and the New Myth of Our Time." Come now, I wanted to say. All that in four weekends?

Moreover, while I had attended enough Pacifica programs to be familiar with a number of their faculty, including adjuncts, I had never heard of the man who would be leading this program. His name was Thomas Elsner. The catalog said he was a certified Jungian analyst and a member of the C. G. Jung Study Center of Southern California as well as a member of the Pacifica faculty. Even though I had attended all those Pacifica programs over the years and had taken a fine course on dream interpretation taught by Jeremy Taylor while I was in seminary, I was far from a devotee of the Swiss psychiatrist Carl Gustav Jung (1875-1961). I barely knew that Jung was the author of *The Red Book*. And though I had been somewhat taken by the poetry of Lord Byron as an undergraduate, the Romantics were not my favorite poets. So why was I drawn to this program?

The description in the catalog did begin to draw me in:

> In the early 20th century, C.G. Jung experienced a crisis of meaning that plunged him into an intensive encounter with the unconscious. One question loomed large: What myth are we living in today? Symbols emerged that pointed to new personal and cultural values gestating in the unconscious. In his recently published *Red Book,* we can see how Jung painted and gave voice to those symbols. ... [E]veryone who gives creative expression to an experience of the unconscious is an alchemist. This intensive will be a vessel for the unfolding of each participant's alchemical opus.

I figured out why I wanted to sign up for Thomas Elsner's intensive. For all I could remember of my early life, and continuing into my 40s, I had been bedeviled by phobias. The fear of looking at a dead body—that fear that might have kept me out of ministry altogether—was one of my phobias. After consulting a whole series of therapists over the years, I had finally marched off long ago to a behavioral therapist who announced that we would devote no time at all to trying to uncover the source of the phobias. Instead, we would stop them from interfering with my life. And so we did—and by the winter of 2015, I had been living many years unhampered by phobias.

But that winter I began saying to myself that before I die, I would like to find out the source of those phobias. I hadn't needed therapy for my phobias for a very long time, but now I longed to understand where they came from. Maybe Thomas Elsner's intensive would help me understand. I signed up.

I was intrigued by the prospect of those four weekends as "a vessel for the unfolding of each participant's alchemical opus." I did know enough about Carl Jung's depth psychology to appreciate the metaphorical description of doing one's own inner work as alchemical. Just as the ancients sought to transform base metals such as lead into gold in a sort of great cooking pot, an alchemical vessel, so might I discover in Thomas Elsner's intensive what spiritual work I needed to do to produce the gold that would be understanding the meaning of my life, hopefully including where those awful phobias came from. It was at least worth a try.

On the airplane to California for the first weekend, I dozed off, and as I awakened, I had one of the dreams that I have come to call my "one-liners." They are common in my dream life. Each one is quite literally one simple sentence that I can write down after I wake up on little more than one line in my dream journal. It often isn't clear in my one-liner dreams who, if anybody, is saying the words or whether they simply appear in writing. In any case, I awakened from my airplane nap to these words: "Alan will be coming soon."

To be sure, these were startling words. They did not frighten me, however. I simply didn't know what to make of them. Since there was much else on my mind as I made my way from the Los Angeles airport north to Santa Barbara and then up the hill to Pacifica Graduate Institute, the one-liner floated away. It came back with a jolt when I walked into the classroom that Friday evening where Thomas Elsner stood at the lectern ready to begin the first session of our four-weekend intensive. I sat down quickly. In front of me, complete with body language and facial expressions I had not seen for almost twenty years, there in essence was Alan.

It took almost no time for Thomas Elsner to have our group of about twenty-five people at ease, calling him Tom and sharing hopes for the weekend, reasons for being there, even dreams. A man sitting near me shared a very revealing dream, which must have emboldened me, because suddenly I was telling about my one-liner and my double take when I walked into the room.

I wrote at the top of the first page of my notes that evening, "Meaning is more important than happiness." Tom Elsner said that. He also said that evening that when I was sitting there and he was speaking, Alan was in the room. Whatever did he mean? Later he started to tell a story and then evidently realized he didn't really want to share that story, at least not at that moment. He stopped himself, saying, "I'll tell you later." If Alan had done that once, he did it a thousand times. I would ask him a question that he didn't want to answer, and he would say, "I'll tell you later." After a while I got it that later meant never. Tom, I think, was not being similarly evasive, but his tone and cadence sent me straight to that memory of Alan.

On Sunday morning at the closing session of each weekend of the intensive, we gathered in a semi-circle in front of a fire in the huge fireplace at the corner of our meeting room.Tom invited us then to reflect, first silently in writing or drawing, on what each of us would take home from the weekend. From that first weekend, I found myself paying attention to Tom serving us as more than one sort of person. He was certainly an expert teacher, giving us a wealth of information and ideas about the depth psychology of Carl Jung and also drawing us out. But at the same time, he brought us his own engaged and enlightened self as a Jungian analyst.

I think even then I had a sense of a significant difference between a Jungian analyst and a psycho-therapist. I understood then, and still do, that the latter seeks to cure some ailment with the goal of wellness, while the former serves as guide and companion through the dark wilderness of the unconscious in search of wholeness, bringing outer and inner into fruit-ful relationship with each other. From the beginning, it seemed to me that Tom was being with us at least in part as such a guide and companion.

I kept thinking about how those four weekends were described in the Pacifica catalog not as a "class" or a "program" but as an "intensive." And sure enough, we participants were not simply students in a class taking in information. Tom clearly was inviting each of us to be present to whatever might be our own alchemical work, not just any old task but our magnum opus. That first Sunday morning he described our circle as an alchemical cooking vessel. The alchemical opus is to hold whatever it is that we don't know in suspension, or as the poet John Keats would have it in his theory of negative capability, not to be constantly reaching after reason, not making knowledge or facts the primary thing. Instead, the alchemical opus invites being attentive to— but not trying too soon to resolve—emotions, conflicts, or whatever it is that we don't know. Our group had three more weekends ahead of us, three more months to practice holding things in suspension.

Throughout the intensive, Tom drew upon the processes of Jungian analysis. He gave us many opportunities to share our dreams. He invited us to enter into active imagination with our dreams, not trying to explain or interpret them, but entering into dialogue with dream figures or expressing them through drawing. He showed us pages from Jung's *Red Book,* the great collection of intricate and beautiful mandalas that Jung drew when he engaged in active imagination with his own dreams. Tom invited us to pay attention to especially vivid images in our dreams. He said they might serve us by pointing to something important in our unconscious that we might come to understand if only we would be patient, not rush, and hold things in suspension.

I am no longer sure when it was that seeking the source of my phobias stopped being the main purpose of my being in that intensive. I am no longer sure how Alan grew so insistent in his knocking on the wall of my unconscious. A couple of days before I flew back to California for the March weekend of the intensive, he piped up in another one-liner dream, saying, "I gather you don't know I'm here." By then I was at least beginning to get it.

At the end of that weekend, on the bus ride south from Santa Barbara to the airport, I suddenly saw outside the window a military cemetery, row upon row of white headstones, going this way and that, up this knoll, down that slope, row upon row, beyond those trees, across that road, everywhere, filling the whole picture of the world until there was no place where they were not.

At the Sunday morning session on the final weekend of the intensive, Tom invited us each to find a quiet place alone on the beautiful Pacifica campus to write or draw for a little while before our group's final time of sharing with each other. What had our time together meant to us? What would we take home when we left for the last time? As usual, I was inclined more to write than to draw. But in my mind's eye, I saw the many things I wrote down as a patchwork quilt. By then there were many pieces in my quilt. It started with that one-liner dream, "Alan will be coming soon," and how that dream over the spring came to mean so much more to me than any wish I had to discover the source of my old phobias. Several other participants in the intensive were prominent pieces of the quilt as were some guest presenters and even some authors we had read.

At the center of the quilt, without doubt, was Tom Elsner. In my reflections that morning, I wrote of my heartfelt sense of him as a teacher, holding the group, managing the dynamics of the people in it, finding ways to convey masses of material so that we could take it in and make something of it.

But I realized that from the beginning I had been paying attention to Tom as a Jungian analyst also. I knew that the essence of successful analysis depends on the relationship between analyst and analysand, that the one must be caring companion and guide to the other as they travel together through the dark wilderness of the unconscious in search of whatever gifts of meaning might be found there. That final weekend, in the Pacifica bookstore I had come across a book called *Bridge Work* by my former student Dennis Patrick Slattery (Slattery, 2015), the one who was responsible for my discovering Pacifica in the first place. I had been reading Dennis's book in my room on Saturday evening and came upon his reflection on the poet Rainer Maria Rilke's responses to letters from a young aspiring poet. For Dennis, the responses, taken together, carry this message: "Our life depends on engaging what beckons. It is a summons to meaning..."

After the final session of the intensive, I asked Tom Elsner if he would work with me long-distance on Skype, doing Jungian analysis. He said he would.

For a time then, Alan lay low, while, with a lot of help from my dreams, Tom and I dug into my family history, my mercurial professional life, and my early brief and altogether unsatisfactory marriage.

But then one day I came across a mystifying poem by someone named Irena Klepfisz called "Dedications to Bashert." (Klepfisz, 2006) The poem has two parts. The first part is headed: "*These words are dedicated to those who died."* After listing many reasons why some people died, that part of the poem concludes with that word I did not know—"Bashert." The second part of the poem is headed: *"These words are dedicated to those who survived."* After listing many reasons why some people survived, that part also concludes—"Bashert." It was not lost on me that in the poem some of the same reasons that some people survived were also reasons that other people died, and some of the same reasons that some people died were also reasons that other people survived. Some people died because they took risks, and others survived because they took risks. Some people survived because they played it safe, and others died because they played it safe.

I had to find out what that mysterious word "Bashert" means. I learned it is a Yiddish word. In general, it can be applied to anything that is "meant to be." When I found out that Irena Klepfisz is a Holocaust survivor, I was concerned that I not appropriate the powerful message of her poem if she meant it to be exclusively about those who died in the Holocaust and those who survived. It was a relief to me to read what she said in an interview, "I've been told that those two dedications have been read for gay men who died of AIDS. They were included in a gay and lesbian oratorio. They've also been included in endless Passover Haggadahs and all kinds of Jewish and non-Jewish rituals." (Pacernick, 2001) And it seemed to me right, when I read in an essay about both Klepfisz's artistry and her activism, that the poem's dedications to "those who died" and then to "those who survived" at least "allow the reader to translate between past and present traumas." (McTaggart, 2007) It was not out of bounds then for me to read that poem as being dedicated also to those who were casualties of the Vietnam War and those who survived.

Lexicographers mention that "Bashert" is sometimes said of couples who were meant to be together, soul mates, you might say. The lexicographers are quick to point out that being meant to be together does not necessarily mean being meant to be happy together, or being happy at all. And Irena Klepfisz has associated "Bashert" with "predestination, inevitability, a sense of finality, hopelessness, inexplicability." (Pacernick, 2001) "Meaning is more important than happiness," Tom Elsner had said.

After I read "Dedications to *Bashert*" and began to ponder the meaning of both dying and surviving, it was no longer the case that Alan would be coming soon. He was most definitely here, demanding that I wake up, commanding me to pay attention, find things out, maybe even write them down. And then someone showed me a picture of a stone that has become part of the Vietnam War Memorial at Odessa, Texas. It turns out that the words etched on that stone have been quoted often, but no one seems to know who was the wise person who first wrote them down. My guess is that it was a Vietnam veteran, somebody who came home and survived, at least long enough to write the words that are now etched on the stone at the Odessa, Texas, War Memorial: "Not everyone who lost his life in Vietnam died there. Not everyone who came home from Vietnam ever left there."

My work with Tom Elsner took a definitive turn then. My alchemical opus was to search out the meaning of my relationship with Alan and what it had to tell me about the meaning of my life. I still didn't know, however, that my alchemical opus would turn out to call forth writing this book.

Chapter 6

Digging Deeper

The path into the light seems dark,
the path forward seems to go back,
the direct path seems long…

—from *Tao te Ching*, 41
trans. Stephen Mitchell

There has long been a black pocket-folder in one of the file cabinets in my home study labeled simply "Alan." I suppose it has been there ever since at least shortly after he died, when I must have begun right away to collect things that I wanted to be sure not to lose track of. I have always been able to remember at least some of what's in that folder, though I could never come close to naming everything there. One day after an hour with Tom Elsner, I decided I needed to open up the folder and see what I might find. I thought of what I was about to do as excavation. I was going to dig a tunnel down and further down, to see what I might unearth. Some things near the surface I knew I would find—my "Open Letter to a Vietnam Veteran," the orders of service for the memorial gatherings in Gainesville and Kent, the plastic bag.

I knew I would find in the folder the plastic bag in which Enid Morris, Alan's mother, brought his ashes to the cottage the day we scattered them in the Santa Fe River. It turned out that she'd also had her beloved cat cremated and she'd put the cat's ashes along with some of Alan's ashes in the plastic bag. I was horrified by what seemed to me a desecration of Alan's body, but there was nothing I could do about it, so somehow I convinced myself not to let it ruin what we were there to do.

And then it turned out that I forgot all about the cat when Enid cast some of Alan's ashes into the river. She spoke aloud then to Alan as the little boy she would far rather remember than the mysterious, fierce, unpredictable, tormented man he had become.

A vet buddy of Alan's named Kevin Sullivan had written a song for Alan. Down on the dock, Kevin sang his song and played his guitar. His friend Bill came along. Bill was another vet who suffered from the effects of exposure to Agent Orange. He had the same *porphyria cutanea tarda* that I had seen destroying the skin on Alan's hands. Bill threw his fistful of ashes into the river with an angry shout.

The breeze caught the ashes and they swirled in the air. They sparkled in the summer sunshine and made me think of gold dust and made me think that some little molecule of Alan might somehow get lodged somewhere in the dock and would maybe still be there whenever I went down there to sit and watch the movement of the water and the sun.

I know how much it pleased me when I read all these years later that "[w]hen a man dies, and is cremated, and his ashes are given to the sea, some of his molecular and atomic integrity remains 'extant,' as biologists say carefully—which is to say that many of the atoms of which he was composed do not dissolve, but rather enter other forms and beings." (Doyle, 2016) It was an article about the life and death of the guitar player John Mellor, better known as Joe Strummer of the Clash. After he died, his daughters put his ashes into the Alboran Sea, where the atoms of which he had been composed were swept into the ocean where they could well have entered fish and other creatures. Brian Doyle concludes, "Some of him entered fish that entered people, one of whom may be you." And so perhaps my idea of some molecule of Alan remaining there under the dock was not so fanciful after all. And so also even a biologist might agree that it was not impossible for something of Alan's very self to enter me at some unknown time, even long after our ceremony on the dock.

After my friend Gail Collins-Ranadive read this passage, she sent me something that has been reprinted often under the title "Eulogy from a Physicist." It concludes: "According to the law of the conservation of energy, not a bit of you is gone; you're just less orderly." (Freeman, 2005) I smiled when I read that, and I could hear Alan guffawing somewhere off in the distance.

I knew I would find that plastic bag in the folder. I didn't know what I would do when I found it. What I did was hold it up to the light to see if there were any particles still there. There were. I looked at them through the plastic for a long time. When I held up the bag, they skittered around inside. I guess I knew all along that eventually I would open the bag and stick my nose in to discover what it would smell like, and I did that. It just smelled dry and old. It might as well have been dusty old newspaper in there. And then with really no further thought, I stuck my hand in and went all the way to the bottom where the particles were, and then I brought my hand out and smelled it. Nothing. And then I rubbed my two hands together for any feel of grit or dust or anything. Nothing. If Alan was truly gone from that bag, well then, so was Enid's cat. I folded the bag back up, pressed the air out of it, put it back where I found it, and went on excavating the contents of the folder.

I found what I had written for the Memorial Garden Book at the Unitarian Universalist Church of Tampa. This is the church I was called to serve after my year as an interim minister at the Sepulveda Unitarian Universalist Society in the San Fernando Valley of Los Angeles. While I was serving the Tampa church, the congregation decided to create a Memorial Garden. A member who was a wonderfully creative artist named Carol Chaney volunteered to design a memorial stone for any deceased person that any of us wanted to have included. The memorial stones were flat round pavers, laid out in a large circle in the beautifully wooded church yard. There was no gravestone for Alan anywhere, and I was grateful for the opportunity to have a stone for him in the Tampa church's Memorial Garden. The congregation decided to have a notebook where we could write about the person for whom we had a stone placed in the garden.

No one in the Tampa church had known Alan. He had died a little over a year before I went there to serve. The Memorial Garden notebook gave me a chance to let people there know at least something of him. I wrote about how we met, about his service in Viet Nam, his life, and his death. I wrote about how during the years we were together, I watched the war relentlessly taking its toll on him. I wrote about what a powerful act of courage I thought it was for him to take part in the Winter Soldier encampment in Washington and throw his Purple Heart into the heap of medals veterans tossed away. I wrote how happy I was that in the final years of his tortured life he became active in the Gainesville Chapter of Veterans for Peace. And finally, I mentioned that he ended his life at a cottage on the Santa Fe River in North Florida that he greatly loved. My note in the Memorial Garden Notebook ended this way:

> Alan taught me much—about loving and living and dying and war and peace. The Christmas after his death, the Gainesville Veterans for Peace named their annual holiday concert as a memorial for him. The Vets for Peace logo is a dove with a ribbon its mouth, and I will always be glad that the one visible memorial to Alan anywhere is the stone in the Memorial Garden at the Unitarian Universalist Church of Tampa, with its beautiful design of a dove with a ribbon in its mouth.

I remembered well enough at least in a general way what Alan's memorial stone looked like, patterned after the Vets for Peace logo, but I also knew I had no actual picture of it, and I knew I wanted one. I looked up contact information for the current minister of the Tampa church, someone I did not know named Rev. Patricia Owen, who was soon to be installed there during the congregation's sixtieth year. I sent her a message, extending best wishes for both the church's anniversary and her installation. And I asked her the favor of taking a picture of Alan's stone and sending it to me.

In no time I had a note back from her with five pictures of the stone attached. I caught my breath when the first picture appeared on my computer screen. There was Carol Chaney's beautiful artistry, the many iridescent chips in shades of blue and in the center the white dove with a black ribbon in its mouth. The stone ring around the outside had darkened in the 15 years since Carol etched "Alan G. Morris" into it, but I could still read it well enough.

Memorial stone for Alan G. Morris in the Memorial Garden at the Unitarian Universalist Church of Tampa, Florida. Photograph by Patricia Owen. With permission.

Patricia Owen sent me eight pictures in all that afternoon. But she did more than that. She told me that she read what I wrote about Alan in the Memorial Garden notebook. And she wrote back that she was a veteran herself with 22 ½ years of service beginning with Desert

Storm. She wrote to me, the former minister of the church she was serving: "I am glad part of Alan's spirit is resting here—I am, all at one time, a conflicted veteran and a veteran with great pride. I don't leave my comrades ... so knowing a little more about him strengthens my resolve. In faith, P"

Many people have a quotation that follows their signature at the end of every email. Patricia Owen's quotation is from James Luther Adams: "A living tradition is not bequeathed through some law of inheritance. It must be earned, not without dust and heat, and not without humbling grace."

When I wrote to thank Patricia for the pictures and her message to me, I said, "It touches me deeply to think that you, a veteran who understands these terrible complexities, are there. Alan's spirit will rest easier there now, I think, and I will rest easier too."

By the time of my correspondence with Patricia Owen, I had been spending three or four hours a month in conversation on Skype with Tom Elsner, and I had been writing more and more in my journal about Alan. It had become increasingly clear that my excavations were not simply to unearth more facts about him. The work—my work—was not just about him. It was about us. And as I had written to him all those years ago, I truly could not tell his story, only he could do that. The story I had to tell was my own, and with Tom Elsner's help, I was well into it.

There was an unexpected stroke of luck—or synchronicity—in all this.It turned out that one of my professional organizations held a meeting at a retreat center outside of Santa Barbara, and this meant that for

Digging for fossils.

one hour, I actually got to sit down in Tom's office and talk with him face-to-face, with no frequently blurring computer screen or freezing audio separating us. That day, something prompted me to tell him of my memories of swimming down the Ichetucknee River, with Alan waiting for me, propped against a tree in the park near where that river empties into the Santa Fe. It was a summertime story. This was not the Alan just about ready to take himself out. It was early on in our time together. The tree still had life in it, branches and leaves.

When I was telling this, looking at Tom, there was a conflation of images for me. I was not sure about Tom's age, but I guessed he was in his late 40s, about the age Alan was when he died—47. The Alan propped against the tree was some years younger, not so gray, much more agile. And so, when I looked at Tom, I

Alan Morris   Tom Elsner, with permission.

wondered if what I was seeing was the Alan that Alan
never got to be, a healthy, vibrant Alan, one with humor
that was not biting and sardonic, one clear of eye and
steady of hand. I never have dreams about Alan. He
does not disturb my sleep with orders and commands.
But three or four times a month, and that one Thursday
very much in person, Alan has been with me, smiling,
able to pay attention and to respond. It seems to me
now that my one-liner dream on the airplane was an
annunciation, an announcement: "Alan will be coming
soon." Annunciations, it seems to me, don't lie.

When I read to Tom later my reflection on his
embodying the Alan that Alan never got to be, he told
me that he was then 49, so I was not far off. And when
I shared with him my writing about that dream being an
annunciation, he said he thought it was meant to be

that I took the Pacifica class and that it led to him companioning me on this journey, this excavation. That is when I started thinking that if all this turned out to be a book, it was important to me for him to be in it, too. If I had any doubt about that, it went away when I read an interview with the psychotherapist Gary Greenberg, in which he said:

> The really valuable part of therapy isn't what you learn about the effects of what your parents did to you, your conflict with your boss, or your broken heart. Freud said that psychoanalysis is a "cure through love," and I think that is essentially correct. The love is conveyed not so much in the content as in the form: the rapt attention of someone who cares enough to interrogate you. The love stows away in the conversation.... People come to therapy because their life circumstances have somehow disrupted the story they tell themselves about who they are. But even then, the healing isn't only about the new story we fashion. It's about the intimacy. (Greenberg, 2016)

Chapter 7

Bringing Forth

If you bring forth what is within you,
what you bring forth will save you.
If you do not bring forth what is within you,
what you do not bring forth will destroy you.

—Gospel of Thomas, 45.30-33
trans. Elaine Pagels

Along with the things I knew I would find in the "Alan" folder—the orders of service, the condolence notes, my "Open Letter to a Vietnam Veteran," and my letter "To Whom It May Concern" in support of Alan's stressor letter to the VA—I found something else that at first completely mystified me. It was a list of questions on white lined three-hole paper torn out of a notebook. The questions were written in a handwriting I did not recognize, certainly neither Alan's nor mine, though phrased as though I had written them.

Why did I choose him?
Why did I stay?
Why did he choose me?
Why <u>that</u> night?

The list went on to ask what he really felt for me, why he liked guns so much, how much the war was responsible for his death and how much the responsibility lay with who he was. The final questions:

Was all this inevitable?

What am I to do?

And at the bottom of the page, with no punctuation:

no answers

But who wrote all this and phrased the questions as if I had asked them? An attached page provided at least the possibility of an explanation. It contained some notes on EMDR (Eye Movement Desensitization and Reprocessing), a therapy technique for treating trauma. EMDR was getting a lot of attention in the 1990s as a new and, according to some, dramatically successful method for relieving PTSD. I remembered wondering whether it could give Alan some relief, and then I also remembered going to a therapist myself to try it out. Whether I had done this before or after Alan's death, I wasn't sure until I read that list of questions. My experiment must have happened after Alan's death. I wasn't there to see whether I wanted to urge Alan to try EMDR. I was there to try it as therapy for my own stress in the wake of his death. And the therapist must have written down questions that I expressed out loud. After the question, "Why that night?" surely referring to his suicide happening on the night of my graduation from seminary, the writer wrote between the lines "Rebecca?"

Rebecca? Who was Rebecca? At first the name meant nothing to me. But soon it all came back—the remains of two take-out dinners that I found in the cottage refrigerator when I went back in there for the first time after Alan's death, and the condolence note, which was also buried in the file. The words printed on the card said:

No words could ever tell you
the feeling of deep sympathy
this brings to you today.

In her own handwriting, she had added:

I don't know you but I believe you to be a strong & beautiful woman. I wish I could answer the question but I can't. Take care of yourself
Rebecca

The question had to be why Alan shot himself that night. Or maybe it was two questions—why he shot himself at all and why he did it that night. For Rebecca, that had to be a different question from mine. If I asked why he shot himself while I was graduating from seminary, she surely asked why he did it while she was there in the cottage with him. She called me up one day shortly afterwards, this woman that I didn't know existed. She told me she was in the bathroom when she heard the shot. I told her that I was sure she needed help and comfort in the wake of that experience but that she would have to find that help and comfort somewhere else. I could not give her what she needed.

There were so many questions I could have asked her—about that night, about their relationship, about how long it had been going on and how close it was and what he meant to her, if anything at all. But I could not ask those questions. All I could think of was that this woman whose existence I had never even known of, experienced the very thing that I grew weak in the knees with relief knowing that I had not had to experience. She saw Alan dead. She knew what it was like to see a person who had put a Colt .45 to his own head and pulled the trigger. It was a sure thing that when she went to that cottage with that man that night, she had no idea that was going to happen. Did she know it was my cottage? Did she know I existed? Surely none of that mattered to her any more, if it ever had. And then I could not think of a reason why it should matter to me either.

Eventually I found in the "Alan" folder, in his hand-written phone log, a phone number for Rebecca and a last name to go with it. I thought about trying to call her, but then I thought better of it. There was no good reason to bring to her mind a whole lot of memories that she most probably did not want to revisit. And if she had anything to contribute to the meaning I sought, it was not to be found in details but in the one simple fact that she was present in that cottage on a particular night twenty years before and in Alan's life for some unknown period of time before that night.

Thinking about Rebecca brought back to my mind another woman whose name I never knew and whom I also never saw, but whom I never, not for one instant, ever forgot. I have always referred to her in my thoughts as "the jewelry thief." Until I mentioned her to Tom Elsner, I had never mentioned her to anyone, not even to Alan, that is, not after the night I learned of her existence.

Here is what happened. One weekend while I still lived in Gainesville, I went off to a church women's conference in Orlando. When I returned home on Sunday evening, Alan was at my house. He said we should go out for dinner, and for some reason he was keen on my not going into my bedroom before we got into the car. This, of course, only made me more certain that I did want to go in there. It turned out that he had brought a woman there that weekend and she had stolen some of my jewelry. I don't know when Alan discovered the theft or how. But he was certain that as soon as I discovered it, it would mean the end of our relationship. He was hoping we might have the pleasure of one peaceful dinner together before I kicked him out of my life.

What I remember is that we did have dinner in a restaurant that evening, that we were deadly silent, anything but peaceful, but that, above all, I did not end our relationship. And it continued over the years to be my guilty secret that I didn't end it, putting my self-respect in serious and unremitting jeopardy. When I remember that evening, it always brings back to me our first night together and how it was absolutely essential to him that we have a few drinks at a bar before he came to my house. Alan Morris needed somebody drunk, as anesthetized as he was, to have sex. That way, nobody had to take feelings into account.

I think about how whenever I worked up the courage to ask him to tell me he loved me, his answer inevitably was that he did not have feelings. Still, we were in some kind of relationship, however inexplicable, years after I quit drinking, years after he took a jewelry thief into my bed, and even while he was also having some kind of relationship that surely involved sex with a woman named Rebecca who turned out to be destined to come out of the bathroom in the cottage one night and encounter him just after he put the revolver to his head and pulled the trigger.

Learning of Rebecca's presence in my cottage that night—and of her very existence—was much less shocking than it might have been because I had carried the memory of the jewelry thief in my head all those years. And if I had only thought of it, I might have surmised that between the jewelry thief and Rebecca, there was likely a string of other women, long or short. It didn't matter. *Bashert*. We were bound together by a thread that no such circumstances had the power to break.

Which still leaves unanswered the question why this was so, why such an unlikely pair as the two of us stayed bound to each other as we did through all those years and why over two decades after Alan's death, I know in my bones that the Alan in me still has much to tell me about who I am.

I have been thinking about how it is that I have regarded my relationship with Alan as intimate. I know that many times I have characterized it that way to others, both before and even long after his death. How could I say such a thing when this was a man who never said to me the words, "I love you," never called me "honey" or "darling" or any other term of endearment, never gave me a hug or held my hand when we walked somewhere side by side? Amazing as this is when I think about it now, I don't remember Alan ever kissing me on the mouth. Can this be so?

I can call forth the image of sitting next to him in a bar and having him put his hand on my shoulder and whisper something in my ear. At such moments, what would he have whispered? Not "sweet nothings," surely. More likely he was making some snide comment about someone across the room, and he didn't want that person to hear him. Or maybe he was telling me a joke and would quietly guffaw at the end. I remember that when he was in Ponce Inlet and I was in Gainesville, back in the years before I quit drinking, while there was still plenty of sexiness between us, he would call me up and ask me to "talk dirty" to him. Even back then, when I was likely drunk myself, that request made me uncomfortable. I didn't know what to say.

The pictures of us at the Alachua County fair were pictures of an early Alan and Barbara, drunk, teasing, with our sexiness breaking out in full force. We quite certainly were enjoying each other, and enjoying ourselves in each other's company. But we had not been together very long at that point. Would "intimate" have described our relationship then? I don't think so.

In fact, how ironic it is that I now believe the intimacy between us developed and grew deeper only later when my drinking and much of our sex life were things of the past. Whatever does this mean? How can this be so?

I think it has to do with our being quiet with each other. Drunk and all sexed up, we were anything but quiet. I have written before about how much I loved our quiet times together—our long rides in silence in either the car or the boat, the night we sat for a long time in silence surrounded by fireflies. But I also wrote that

Alan's was a busy silence behind his fierce and faraway face. If he was truly somewhere else—back in Viet Nam most likely—how can I possibly characterize those times together as indicative of an intimacy between us?

The "Alan" file is not the only significant one in my file cabinet. One day I came across the records of my Career Assessment, a psychological evaluation process required of candidates for credentialing as Unitarian Universalist ministers. One question asked us candidates to pick among five options which best described our "present marital/relationship situation." I checked the middle option: "neither satisfactory nor unsatisfactory." The follow-up question directed: "Describe your present relationship with your partner." I wrote:

> He lives in Florida. We talk on the phone on the average once every week or two. I will spend a week with him in January. Our lives are very different, yet we enjoy the time we spend together at my cottage in Florida. He is less demonstrative than I would like and generally uncommunicative about feelings. He suffers from post-traumatic stress syndrome from the Vietnam War, which takes a toll on our relationship, yet I enjoy quiet time with him.

I filled out this questionnaire late in the fall of 1993, late in my first semester in seminary in Berkeley.

On December 27 of that same year, a staff psychologist at the VA in Gainesville wrote his report of a consultation with Alan to assess whether he should be referred for therapy for PTSD. This report, which did conclude with the diagnosis of PTSD, turned up in my "Alan" file. It included this:

> Patient has been involved in a number of close relationships over the years which have been maintained for rather extended periods but stopping short of full commitment. At present he has separated from a woman with whom he was attached for the past five years. This relationship became tenuous and is in the process of final dissolution because of his increasing anxiety problems.

I read this multiple times to make sure I had not misread it. No, I read it right. It says Alan reported that his relationship with me had been going on five years at that point, not the actual seven, and that he had separated from me. It says he reported that our relationship had become "tenuous" and that it was "in the process of final dissolution." I took a deep breath. I was tempted to discount the whole report since it was written by somebody who misspelled Alan's name and wrote that he went to school at Penn State instead of Kent State. Why should I trust this psychologist to get anything right?

But after all, I could not get off the hook that easily. I suppose I could wonder whether Alan didn't tell the psychologist the truth but instead said whatever he thought would be most likely to get him the PTSD diagnosis he needed. But then I would have to ask whether *I* told the unvarnished truth when I filled out my Career Assessment questionnaire.

We each wanted something. He wanted to be found fit for PTSD treatment. I wanted to be found fit for ministry. We each knew that what we said might well have bearing on whether we got what we wanted. In any event, neither the psychologist who assessed him nor the one who assessed me would likely have concluded that our relationship was an intimate one; neither would have likely predicted that it would continue for 2 ½ more years until it ended with Alan's death.

It takes my breath away now when I think about all this. My Career Assessment questionnaire and the psychologist's report of his consultation with Alan were both written at just about the same time I wrote my "Open Letter to a Vietnam Veteran," in which I poured out my heart to him and committed myself to staying with him for the long haul. It may be telling that I have no memory whatsoever of any response from Alan to that letter. I'm sure there was no written response. He never wrote me letters. But surely, he *said* something about it. After all, we were together for his birthday on January 10, the very next month after all those writings—my Career Assessment questionnaire, the psychologist's report, and my Open Letter.

I suppose someone could make a good case that everything I have said about intimacy between us is a fiction, that I made it all up, that it was nothing more than wishful thinking on my part, that I created out of whole cloth a relationship that never existed except in my fantasies. Yes, I suppose there is a good case to be made. This was a man who was so damaged by what he could not forget from the war that he was truly unable to experience feelings at all, that he lived for a quarter of a century after the war in a state of complete anesthetization, and that, therefore, it really didn't matter to him that I chose to go away to school at the other end of the country. And it didn't matter whether some kind of relationship with me would continue or whether it wouldn't.

That bullet in his brain 2 ½ years later may well have happened during a game of Russian roulette with his newly purchased Colt .45. If one spin of the revolver didn't finish him off, well, the next one would, or the one after that. What difference did it make how many spins it took? A good case could be made for all of this. An intimate relationship with me, with anyone? What a laugh!

Thinking about all this prompted me to track down Suzanne Autumn, the friend who told me on the phone of Alan's death. She moved away from Gainesville soon afterwards, and I had not been in touch with her for most of the twenty years since. When I emailed her, I mentioned how grateful I was for her thoughtfulness when she made that phone call. It had never really come home to me what a hard phone call that had to be for her to make. She told me it was the hardest thing she had done in her whole life. She was aware of how much pain she was about to inflict on me, and she had no idea how best to manage it. It felt good to be able to tell her that I was actually grateful to her.

I think I may have removed from her shoulders a burden she had been carrying for twenty years. Suzanne knew Alan better than any of my other Gainesville friends. She visited us at the cottage sometimes, and I remember that once she had Christmas dinner with us there. Still, when she and I talked on the phone these decades later, she said something that I never knew was her impression. She said she knew that Alan and I were kindred souls. In a curious way, having her say that was a kind of confirmation that it was true. *Bashert.*

But then I had a flash of new memory—a memory that the day after my seminary graduation in Berkeley, I flew from the Bay Area down to the San Fernando Valley to interview for a position as interim minister at the Sepulveda Unitarian Universalist Society. If that was so, then I surely knew before I left Florida for California that weekend that I was not getting the Florida District Executive's position. When did I find that out? Surely long enough before that weekend to have arranged for the interview with the Sepulveda search committee. And if I knew, did I tell Alan? Did we both know that when he stuck his head out the living room door to the porch at the cottage on his way to take his mother to the doctor the last moment I ever saw him?

We did not have a conversation that day. I remember our last conversation, a little while earlier, sitting in the cottage living room. Alan's question came out of nowhere. Would I consider resuming our old relationship? By that he had to mean our sexual relationship, including sleeping together. From some-where came my immediate answer, no, not unless he quit drinking and would agree not to bring loaded weapons into the cottage ever again. Not unless he would go to bed without a loaded pistol within arm's reach. Surely, he knew that. And surely, I knew none of those things was going to happen. But something prompted him to ask all the same. What was that something?

I am left wondering whether I told him that day that I was not getting the position in Florida, and that I would be interviewing for a position in California. Did he know about my changed prospects for the future when he pulled the trigger that Friday night? I have thought a lot about this, and I fervently hope not. For one thing, it must have occurred to me that I might not get the California position after all. But even if I were to get it, I would want us to have as much ordinary time as possible before he knew. It would be like the ordinary time he had hoped to have with me all those years earlier before I discovered a woman had been in my bedroom and stolen some of my jewelry.

I decided not to try to track down Rebecca. But I sent a note to Ruth Gibson, Alan's girlfriend during his time in Kent, inviting her to have a conversation with me about him. It was a clunky note, not the gracious and polished one I'd hoped to send. It was handwritten on a card with a drawing of blue birds on the front. As I struggled for the right words, I kept thinking I should have written the note on the computer so I could edit before sending. But that would have seemed almost as calculated as if I had paid $20 to some people-tracking outfit to track down with more certainty her current address and phone and maybe even more besides. I was not launching an investigation; I was inviting a conversation.

So, I sent off the card to the address on Alan's phone log that also gave a phone number that the phone company told me was no longer in service. That same piece of yellow paper had a listing for me also with my Berkeley phone number. I was listed as "B.A. Child." Ruth was listed as "Ms. R.G.," but underneath in one of the few instances of long-hand writing I have ever seen from Alan other than his signature, he had written "Ruthie." I never heard him call her that.

I wrote "Please forward" on the envelope and sent off my card. It remained to be seen how long I would wait for a response or my card to be "returned to sender" before I would decide whether to go the people-tracking route, after all, or let the whole matter drop.

When I had called the phone number that turned out to be out of service, I made no plan ahead of time about what I would say. I had no written list of questions. What, after all, did I want to know from Ruth? Did I want to know whether the Alan she loved was different from the Alan I loved? Did I want to know what attracted her to him? Were they magnetized too? Could someone have said of them, "*Bashert*—they were destined for each other"? After all, do the answers to any of these questions matter?

They are questions of fact; they probably have little if anything at all to do with meaning. For a while, I thought it was essential that I talk to Ruth, and maybe even Rebecca too, before I could conclude my excavation and bring forth whatever of Alan was to be found within me. But now I no longer think so. Ruth and Rebecca might be able to give me some facts I don't have, but neither of them can provide the code to unlock the mystery of the meaning of Alan's presence in almost half a century of my conscious and unconscious life.

I do know this. In a very real sense, that bullet did not end Alan's life. I am still here. I am still working out the meaning of my life, and my relationship with Alan continues to be *prima materia* in the alchemist's vessel. And in a way which remains no less true simply because I cannot explain it, I remain sure that we were meant to be together. Maybe we were meant to be together so that after that bullet did its work, I could take up the work of sharing what I know of Alan's story with other people, so that other people could no longer escape knowing the truth about that war—any war—and its effects on human beings, both those who go to war and somehow manage to keep on living, at least for a time, afterward, and those who stay with them during that time of living afterward. And now I know how to say that being together during that time of living afterward is best described as intimate. *Bashert.*

The night after I thought through all these things, I could not sleep. I slept almost not at all. I spent a lot of time in the darkness trying without success to conjure up Alan's face—not the face in any of the many photos I have of him but his actual face with any of the expressions that were common there. And in the night's silence I tried with no more success to conjure up the sound of his voice saying any of the things he often said, any of the turns of phrase that were distinctively his. Try as I might, I could not bring to mind a single one of them.

I began to cry, just as I had the day before when I heard on the radio a song called "I Will Wait" by Mumford & Sons. Try as I might, I could not hear Alan's voice, but I could hear over and over, with increasing insistence and volume, "I will wait. I will wait for you." And finally, I realized these were not Alan's words but my own.

Why did those words make me cry? I certainly have not been expecting a visitation from some ghost. Alan has not been present in my dreams, and I truly was not holding out some hope that he would show up there. What then? What exactly did I think I was waiting for, and why did professing it bring me to tears? And why did I choose that word "professing"? We speak of a profession of faith. It is more than a statement. It is a commitment. Just as, all those years ago, I put back on my finger the ring Alan had given me and that I had taken off during my time of wavering, waiting to discover whether I would remain committed to him or not, so now I profess that I will not give up my quest for meaning.

Not long ago, I read an interview with Barry Svigals, the lead architect in the firm engaged to build a new school building on the site where the people of Newtown, Connecticut, razed the Sandy Hook Elementary School. A gunman had shot and killed twenty children and six adults there on December 14, 2012. Svigals explained to the interviewer that the architects' focus needed not to be on what the building would look like but instead on what the people there needed. "The most important tool," he said, "is to remember that we don't know—an active not-knowing." (Svigals, 2016) I believe Barry Svigals' advice is good, not just for the architectural team in Newtown, Connecticut. I believe it is good advice for everybody. In any case, I know it is good advice for me.

More than once Tom Elsner has asked me to reflect on what Alan and I projected onto each other. Those projections surely have something important to do with what drew us to each other. Whatever Alan projected onto me died with him. In other words, the "Barbara in Alan," his anima perhaps, or his shadow, had no existence other than the existence the living Alan gave it. But the "Alan in Barbara," my animus perhaps, or my shadow, has persisted all these years. Whatever it was that drew me to Alan lives on in my unconscious. I cannot call forth his living face or voice. The best I can do is recognize his facial expression or body language in those arresting moments when Tom Elsner embodies them. Maybe it is truly through the love stowed away in my conversations with Tom, as Gary Greenberg would put it, and through Tom's caring interrogations, that my intimacy with Alan may ultimately be shown to me. I know I am not finished waiting for Alan. I know there is more for me to understand, and I need to keep my not-knowing

Photograph by Ruth Gibson, which she put on the cover of the program for the memorial service held at Kent State University, July 6, 1996. With permission.

active. I do not unearth his story exclusively for his sake, or even for the sake of honoring his memory, but also for my own sake. And so, I keep hearing my own voice sing out, "I will wait. I will wait for you."

Epilogue

The Sword and the Snake

On National Public Radio's "Morning Edition," the morning of May 3, 2016, there was a story entitled "How Steel from the World Trade Center May Help to Cut Vets' Suicide Rates." A retired Brooklyn firefighter and Navy veteran named Danny Prince was telling about driving a load of scraps of steel down to Walter Reed Hospital. The steel scraps came from the wreckage of the World Trade Center. He told how some of the scraps have been made into Stars of David or crosses and welded onto the sides of fire trucks. "You don't want to waste anything," he said.

His buddy Steve Danaluck, who goes by the nickname "Luker," now an American Airlines pilot, formerly a pilot in the Marines, said this steel has a "pure, almost religious nature." It was Luker's idea to take some of that steel and have it forged into a powerful symbol to serve the well-being of veterans. Well, much more than that. To help keep them from killing themselves.

A Texas sword smith melted down the steel and fashioned it into a Greek style sword, short and broad at the tip, the kind of sword famously used by the

Spartan king Leonidas, who fought to the death with his troop of 300 against the huge army of the Persian King Xerxes at the Battle of Thermopylae. Leonidas has been known ever after as the epitome of brave heroism, even against impossible odds.

And so today, the veterans who have formed what they call the Spartan Alliance, bring that Spartan Sword, fashioned from World Trade Center Steel, to groups of veterans whom they invite to take what they call the Spartan Pledge. Veteran Boone Cutler wrote the words, and on my radio that morning, I heard him leading a group of veterans in repeating the words after him: "I will not take my life with my own hand until I talk to my battle buddy first. My mission is to find a mission to help my war fighter family."

Boone Cutler explained that the veteran's worst enemy is isolation. The Spartan Pledge's purpose is to help veterans get connected to somebody they can open up to. Although some therapists and researchers have been skeptical, he is confident the Pledge can work by starting an important conversation.

When the story on my radio finished, I went to my computer. I wanted to see what a Spartan Sword looked like. And sure enough, site after site offered pictures complete with double-edged blade and long point, made for hanging from a baldric under the arm, made for both cutting and thrusting during close combat. I learned I could buy a replica from Amazon for $38.72. Even better, an outfit called BUDK was having a close-out: I could save 41% off their regular price and pay only $29.99.

And then I learned that a fighting knife that looked just about like the Spartan Sword was in common use in Viet Nam, not issued by the government but privately purchased by U.S. soldiers. It was easy to conceal. It lent itself to surprise attack. If you were a soldier in Viet Nam, I thought, even though the Army didn't issue you one of these weapons, you would probably be very glad if you had one.

Alan Morris had a tattoo on each upper arm. That morning I looked again at some of my snapshots of Alan. The tattoo on his right upper arm was a Spartan Sword. I don't suppose he ever heard of Leonidas. But I don't know that. I also don't know when or where he got that tattoo. Or why. Which is the question that really matters. Did he own an actual knife styled after a Spartan Sword? My memory has been known to play tricks on me, but I do believe I remember that he had such a knife, that it was sheathed in leather, like the ones available today from Amazon or BUDK. I don't remember ever seeing him use it, though it surely had lots of practical uses outside of combat. But why did he choose to have that blade tattooed on his arm? It was a talisman perhaps. It stood for something. It reminded him of something. I would like to think it reminded him that he could defend himself in close combat if he had to. He was a medic in Viet Nam, after all. It was up to others to conduct offensive operations, not him.

But that morning I heard those veterans on my radio reciting the Spartan Pledge that Boone Cutler, as well as Luker Danaluck and Danny Prince and the others in the Spartan Alliance, hope will keep veterans from committing suicide. If that pledge had been available to

Alan, would he have taken it? Would he have kept it? If there had been a battle buddy for him to call, would he have called, opened up, managed to have a conversation about the things that mattered? And would that conversation have kept him from blasting his brains out with that Colt .45? I don't know. Somehow, I doubt it, but I don't know.

The tattoo on Alan's left upper arm was the coiled snake that these days has come to be the symbol for libertarianism in general, and the National Rifle Association and the Tea Party movement in particular. But these are not 21st century symbols. The coiled rattlesnake on a yellow flag with the words "Don't tread on me" goes back to the Revolutionary War. It is the Gadsden Flag, named for General Christopher Gadsden, who designed it in 1775.

I doubt Alan Morris knew all this. I don't know any more about why he had the Gadsden Flag tattooed on his left arm than I know why he had the Spartan Sword on his right arm. But all the same, I believe there is an appropriateness to that choice he made. Benjamin Franklin published an essay in the *Pennsylvania Journal* in 1775 under the pseudonym "American Guesser," saying that the rattlesnake was an appropriate symbol for the American spirit. He wrote:

> [S]he has no eye-lids—She may therefore be esteemed an emblem of vigilance.—She never begins an attack, nor, when once engaged, ever surrenders.... [T]he weapons with which nature has furnished her, she

conceals in the roof of her mouth, so that, to those who are unacquainted with her, she appears to be a most defenseless animal; and even when those weapons are shown and extended for her defense, they appear weak and contemptible; but their wounds however small, are decisive and fatal:— Conscious of this, she never wounds till she has generously given notice, even to her enemy, and cautioned him against the danger of stepping on her. (www.fi.edu/ga99/musing3)

I think of Alan's vigilance as he walked the perimeter of the property every night at the cottage, just checking on things, before he could possibly lie down and try to sleep. I think of him telling me that sometimes, when I was in Berkeley, he would get in the little boat late at night and row across the river to the cypress swamp on the other side and sit there for hours in that place where he could be just about completely sure no enemy would ever arrive to attack him. Still, he took his rifle with him when he sat there in the cypress swamp, just as he had his pistol under the pillow, or at least no farther away than under the bed, when he did try to go to sleep. I wouldn't be surprised if a short Spartan Sword was nearby as well.

The short Spartan Sword and the coiled rattle-snake—defensive weapons, lethal, always ready, ever vigilant. Alan Morris might not have been able to say why he had those tattoos on his upper arms. But I believe, as talismans, they did their best to keep him safe, keep him alive. Even Leonidas, however, though brave to the end, could not prevail against the onslaught of massive attack. Even the brave, in spite of all their weapons, do sometimes die.

Afterword

In Country

Having loved enough and lost enough,
I'm no longer searching
just opening....

—Mark Nepo
from "Having Loved Enough"

When I told people I was coming to Viet Nam, some responded, "Have a good time." One said, "Have fun." It was clear to me they didn't understand why I had decided to join my friend and ministerial colleague Jan Carlsson-Bull on a pilgrimage led by Edward Tick, scholar, poet, healer, and lover of Viet Nam. Each November since 2000 he has brought here a small group of veterans and loved ones of soldiers killed in the war or otherwise killed by it. I wasn't sure myself why I had decided to join this year's pilgrimage.Alan never had any interest in coming back here. When others told of veterans whose PTSD gave up and left them in peace after they came back, I knew better than to urge him to

157

come. I could just hear him guffawing and see him turning a deaf ear to any such proposal.

And the very idea of my coming here all these twenty-two years after his death? I sometimes say that Alan's spirit resides on the shelf above my desk in my home study. He regularly kibitzes about what appears on my computer screen as I write. The idea of my coming here? Alan's spirit would be guffawing big time. I could hear his voice. "What the hell? What the bloody hell?"

I didn't know why I was coming. The friends who knew better than to wish me a good time or lots of fun did seem to think I must have some particular, identifiable purpose, some mission or goal. And I ought to be able to put it into words and explain it to them. Thank goodness, I discovered Mark Nepo's poem."No longer searching," I was then able to say, "just opening."

Still, I was excited when Ed Tick said we would be able to visit the particular places that figured strongly in Alan's writing about his dust-off missions in the Mekong Delta. We would go to Nui Ba Den, the Black Virgin Mountain, where his helicopter slid backwards down the mountainside in a rainstorm in the dead of night and he was sure they would crash and he would die.We would go to Tan An where he was based during most of his time here "in country." The plan was that I would read his words to our little group of journeying pilgrims in both of these places.

As it happened, Ed Tick's group this year did not include any veterans. It did include four of us women who had lost our beloveds to the war in one way or another.Jan Carlsson-Bull and Billie Knighton had each endured the death of her husband in battle. Lynda Shannon Bluestein and I had endured the effects of the war on the men we loved after they came back home. This year's group also included Julie Davis, Billie's daughter-in-law, who came along to be with her on this pilgrimage and contribute to the continuing healing and growth of their family; Wes Fleming, a chaplain to veterans; Denise McMorrow, a clinical psychologist who treats veterans and their families; and Sebastian Perumbilly, a professor studying the impact of war on family systems of service members. Wes, Denise, and Seb came to learn. The four of us women who had particular places to visit were invited to share with the rest in those places whatever we wished as our chosen form of memorial. I chose to read aloud Alan's words.

Here is what happened.As we neared Nui Ba Den, Ed told us the legend of the lady, dark-skinned from work in the sun in the rice fields, who escaped from marrying someone she did not love. She ran to the mountain and climbed high up and remained there as a Buddhist nun for the rest of her life. I may be wrong, of course, but I doubt that Alan Morris knew anything about the legend of how Nui Ba Den got its name. When we arrived there, it took my breath away to see such a high mountain arising from the plain. We approached not by dust-off helicopter but by funicular. It took nearly half an hour to get up to the lady's pagoda, which was still far below the mountain top.

What I saw when I emerged from the cable car were a large Buddhist pagoda and three other smaller ones including the lady's pagoda. There were refreshment stands and people selling flowers and incense

Reading at Nui Ba Den. Photograph by Jan Carlsson-Bull. With permission.

sticks. Nui Ba Den, with the constant sounds of gong and drum, had become a tourist attraction. Our much loved guide for our entire journey, Tran Dinh Song, found us a space in one of the small pagodas, and though I could still hear gong and drum, I took off my shoes and sat down on the floor. With my journeying companions in a circle around me, I read aloud Alan's words about the helicopter crash in the storm. My companions received my reading with love and appreciation.

The next day we drove to Tan An. My heart leapt when the words "Tan An" began to appear on signs. Tan An is a bustling town, not the little village Song told me it was fifty years ago. We had no idea, of course, where Alan's base had been in relation to the present town. The bus driver stopped the bus near a busy street corner, and we all got out. But it was clear to me that I could not read Alan's words to my companions standing there on that street corner. We got back on the bus. Later on, when we were at our home stay lodging on an island in the Mekong River, I read to them some of Alan's reflections about missions out of Tan An.

On the Mekong River. Photograph by Edward Tick. With permission.

At that point early in our journey, when we were still in the Mekong Delta, I did not yet know that apparently my journey here did have a purpose after all. What I did not yet notice was that I was beginning a spiritual practice—the practice of letting go of expectations. What remained was for me to come to understand what my expectations were.

Ed Tick's annual journeys to Viet Nam are timed to include being here on Veterans Day, more properly termed Armistice Day—the day of achieving and celebrating peace. On Armistice Day we visited three places deemed holy by practitioners of the religions they represent. Two of the three were Buddhist pagodas. The first was the home pagoda of Thich Quang Duc, the monk who famously set himself ablaze in a Saigon intersection in 1963 to protest his government's repression of his religion. The other Buddhist pagoda was the home of probably the most famous Vietnamese peace-making monk, Thich Nhat Hanh, who actually was in residence the day we visited though he was too ill to greet visitors.

At the first Buddhist pagoda, we watched the monks praying for the souls of their departed, and someone told us the names of the dead were being recited in the prayers. Again, as at the pagoda at Nui Ba Den, there was the constant sound of drum and gong. It was a beautiful ceremony, one commanding attention and respect, and I was glad to be there, though I stood far back on the sidelines. This ceremony, I was thinking, had nothing to do with me.

At the conclusion of the ceremony, something happened that I had not expected. Everyone moved outside where at the top of the steps to the courtyard, I suddenly noticed three large bird cages full of very small birds. And then all at once the bird cage doors were opened, and in a great rush the birds flew off together across the courtyard and out of sight. Someone said that through this ritual the souls of the departed were being released from the bonds of earth. I caught my breath. Still, I am not a Buddhist, and this ceremony, I continued to think, had nothing to do with me.

Our other visit on Armistice Day was to a Taoist temple. I especially looked forward to that. I have considered myself something of a Taoist ever since I discovered the *Tao te Ching* when I was studying the world's major religions in seminary. It seemed to me that Lao Tzu, the ancient master of the art of living, asked just the right questions: "Do you have the patience to wait until your mud settles and the water is clear? Can you remain unmoving till the right action arises by itself?" (*Tao te Ching,* 15, trans. Stephen Mitchell)

The day before my appointment with the Unitarian Universalist Association's Ministerial Fellowship Committee, our ministerial credentialing body, I drove down from Berkeley to Big Sur, the area on the California coast that I had come specially to love. I sat with my feet in the Big Sur River and recited the entire *Tao te Ching* out loud. Later someone told me that around Big Sur it is understood that if there is something you need to be rid of, you should let it out of you into the river and the river will carry it away out to sea.

I was looking forward to visiting the Taoist temple right at the edge of the Perfume River outside of Hue. Still, I did a double take when someone there showed us several big bowls of squirming fish. We were each invited to carry a bowl of fish down over the rocks to the water's edge and release the fish into the river. We were told that releasing the fish, like the Buddhists' releasing the birds, would release the soul of our beloved dead from the bonds of earth, from all that had kept that soul in bondage.

What a silly ritual, I was thinking, even as I scooped up a bowl of fish and started making my way down the rocks. The rocks were slippery and my knees were stiff, and those fish took advantage of the circumstances and began wriggling out of the bowl across the rocks. Denise McMorrow, who had helped me down the rocks, now helped me gather up the fish. Suddenly I was flinging that bowl into the air and the fish into the river.

Flinging the fish, and more. Photograph by Wes Fleming. With permission.

And the next thing I knew, I was flinging my own arms high above my head.

It was all about release. At last I knew that this journey has been about release. "No longer searching, just opening." You cannot release anything while you are holding onto it as tightly as ever you can.

In the days before I left for Viet Nam, I became aware of a premonition that I might die here. I tried to slough it off, but I couldn't get rid of it. Maybe I had hold of the idea that if Alan had died here, he would have been spared a quarter century of living as the condemned man he believed he was. Maybe I had hold of some crazy idea that my death here could substitute for his. Somehow or other I was holding on to an idea, a wish, that there was something I could do to change the past.

The day after Jan Carlsson-Bull and I arrived together in Ho Chi Minh City, we visited the huge Saigon open-air market. I have visited such markets before in other cities where many sellers vie for attention and dollars. Nowhere else did this ever bother me. But in that Saigon market, with people constantly calling to me, "Madame," and people constantly tugging at my sleeve, I had to get out of there. I knew at the time that my reaction was extreme, but I couldn't help it. I had to get out of there.

And now I think I know why. I think I was having a flashback to that moment in the midst of a fire fight when the chopper couldn't pull pitch and take off because Vietnamese people were attached like a human chain from the ground up to the door of the chopper and to Alan himself, and the only way he could get his wounded soldier and the pilot and himself out of there was for him to dislodge those fingers and cause those people to drop to their almost certain death.

I have been curious about the theory here that the Vietnamese have no PTSD because, unlike the Americans, they have sorrow and sadness about the past and their losses but neither anger nor wish for revenge. This has been translated into saying they are able to "let it go." The morning after I let those fish go, Ed Tick told us the Buddhist tale of two monks who came across a woman who wanted to cross a stream.

The monks had been taught they were to have no contact with a woman; nevertheless, the older monk picked that woman up and carried her on his back across the stream. After he had put her down on the other side and the two monks had walked on, the younger monk asked the older one why he had done the very thing they had been taught not to do. The older monk answered that he had put that woman down back at the edge of the stream while the younger monk was obviously still carrying her.

I smiled when I realized what Buddhist tale Ed was beginning to tell. I have often told that very tale in sermons on themes related to being stuck in the past. I have called it "wonderful."But that morning on the bus I was questioning that tale, worrying that its message was only superficial, that it glossed over complicated truths.

Later that morning I was interviewed by Seb Perumbilly, our scholar who had come on this journey to learn. He asked me thought-provoking questions about possible differences between Alan before and after the war, about Alan's interactions with other people, about changes in Alan as the years went on, about what being with Alan all those years taught me about war.I tried to answer Seb's questions honestly and in depth. But I found I also wanted to talk about the tale of the two monks and the woman. I wanted to talk about over-simplification and my own insistence on what I sometimes call "complexifying," peeling away layers, attending to details, not risking leaving important things out.

My conversation with Seb that morning finally gave me at least as much as it gave him. I discovered that I still believe the Buddhist tale is wonderful—because I don't believe it is about the act of letting go. I believe letting go is the easy part. The hard part is realizing that you have been holding on tight, that your whole body aches from the strain of holding so much inside. I should have learned this long ago when I first read Lao Tzu: "If you realize that all things change, there is nothing you will try to hold on to." (*Tao te Ching*, 74, trans. Stephen Mitchell)

When I flung those fish into the river, I doubt anything much happened to the soul of Alan Morris. But when I flung my arms in the air, I was the one set free. I used to say to Alan that I could not tell his story. The only story I could tell was my own. Through writing this book, I have at last let loose of it. And I do believe that just as the story of Barbara in Alan was finished when he died, the story of Alan in Barbara is now complete.

Barbara Child
Ha Noi, Viet Nam
November 16, 2018

Acknowledgements

Thanks to Jennifer Fitzgerald, General Manager and Editor at Chiron Publications. I will be forever grateful to her and the others on the Chiron editorial staff for their caring attention to my writing, their responsiveness, and their interest in knowing my thoughts about everything related to publishing this book.

Thanks to my editor, Jan Holloway, whose work shows why even a published author and editor needs an expert editor. Jan's thoughtful and careful attention to my manuscript has made this book immeasurably more readable.

Thanks to Suzanne Autumn, Norma Benavides, Gail Collins-Ranadive, and Amy Jo Smith. They each lived through a part of my story with me, and the book is far better because they read the manuscript and talked with me about what they found in it.

Thanks to Ruth Gibson and Tom Grace. They each lived through part of Alan Morris's story with him, and they are living reminders to me of how suspect is virtually every memory.

Thanks to Ron Mohr and Dennis Patrick Slattery. Without Ron Mohr, the story told in Part One of this book probably would not have happened. Without Dennis Slattery, the story told in Part Two probably would not have happened.

Thanks to *Psychological Perspectives,* the Journal of the C.J. Jung Institute of Los Angeles for permission to publish my "Open Letter to a Vietnam Veteran," which appeared in Vol. 60, No. 1 (March 2017) of that Journal.Special thanks to Margaret O. Ryan, Senior Editor, who suggested I send my manuscript to Chiron Publications.

For Further Reading

What follows is not a comprehensive bibliography but a collection of resources I have found enlightening and thought provoking. I include some notes and quotations that I hope will be helpful in considering which sources to seek out.

War – Accounts from War Correspondents and Veterans

Gloria Emerson and Michael Herr were correspondents in Viet Nam. Chris Hedges served as a war correspondent in Central America, the Middle East, Africa, and the Balkans; he holds a Master of Divinity degree from Harvard University. Sebastian Junger was an embedded reporter in Afghanistan. All four provide firsthand, factual accounts and also reflect on war's causes and effects.

Gloria Emerson. *Winners and Losers: Battles, Retreats, Gains, Losses and Ruins from the Vietnam War*. New York: Harcourt Brace Jovanovich, 1976.

If the children helped the National Liberation Front, they risked punishment, as did any other Vietnamese. If they were caught helping the enemy, there was no one to protect them. Nothing could be done to prepare them to rise above the punishment. It was often a complaint of the American soldiers that the Vietnamese children, whom they found so cute and so lively at first, so pleased to get candy and cigarettes, could not really be trusted. In the swollen, confused cities and near the American bases even the youngest Vietnamese became pimps and thieves. It often angered the soldiers when the children behaved in an ungrateful fashion. Sometimes they did things that led to the sudden death or injuries of the GIs, so even small boys were feared and hated. Many of the soldiers would say this only proved what a lousy country it was because the kids were into the killing. They did not understand that in such a war, children are never left out, that in a country of such huge and dangerous disorders, the children do not stay childlike (pp. 91-92).

Michael Herr. *Dispatches.* New York: Vintage International, 1991.

When I think of it quickly, just seeing the name somewhere or being asked what it was like, I see a flat, dun stretch of ground running out in an even plane until the rim of the middle distance takes on the shapes and colors of jungled hills. I had the strangest, most thrilling kind of illusion there, looking at those hills and thinking about the death and mystery that was in them. I would see the thing I knew I actually saw: the base from the ground where I stood, figures moving across it, choppers rising from the pad by the strip, and the hills above. But at the same time, I would see the other, too; the ground, the troops and even myself, all from the vantage of the hills. It was a double vision that came to me more than once there. And in my head, sounding over and over, were the incredibly sinister words of the song we had all heard for the first time only days before. "The Magical Mystery Tour is waiting to take you away," it promised, "Coming to take you away, dy-ing to take you away..." That was a song about Khe Sanh; we knew it then, and it still seems so (pp. 107-08).

Chris Hedges. *War Is a Force That Gives Us Meaning.* New York: Public Affairs, 2002, 2014.

_____. *What Every Person Should Know about War.* New York: Free Press, 2003.

The myth of war entices us with the allure of heroism. But the images of war handed to us, even when they are graphic, leave out the one essential element of war – fear. There is, until the actual moment of confrontation, no cost to imagining glory. The visual and audio effects of films, the battlefield descriptions in books, make the experience appear real. In fact, the experience is sterile. We are safe. We do not smell rotting flesh, hear the cries of agony, or see before us blood and entrails seeping out of bodies. We view, from a distance, the rush, the excitement, but feel none of the awful gut-wrenching anxiety and humiliation that come with mortal danger. It takes the experience of fear and chaos of battle, the deafening and disturbing noise, to wake us up, to make us realize that we are not who we imagined we were, that war as displayed by the entertainment industry might, in most cases, as well be ballet. ... The prospect of war is exciting. Many young men, schooled in the notion that war is the ultimate definition of manhood, that only in war will they be tested and proven, that they can discover their worth as human beings in battle, willingly join the great enterprise (*War Is a Force That Gives Us Meaning*, pp. 83-84).

Sebastian Junger. *Tribe: On Homecoming and Belonging.* New York: Vintage International, 1991.

_____. *War.* New York: Hachette, 2010.

War is a lot of things and it's useless to pretend that exciting isn't one of them. It's insanely exciting. The machinery of war and the sound it makes and the urgency of its use and the consequences of almost everything about it are the most exciting things anyone engaged in war will ever know. Soldiers discuss that fact with each other and eventually with their chaplains and their shrinks and maybe even their spouses, but the public will never hear about it. It's just not something that many people want acknowledged. War is supposed to feel bad because undeniably bad things happen in it, but for a nineteen-year-old at the working end of a .50 cal during a firefight that everyone comes out of okay, war is life multiplied by some number that no one has ever heard of. In some ways, twenty minutes of combat is more life than you could scrape together in a lifetime of doing something else. Combat isn't where you might die—though that does happen—it's where you find out whether you get to keep on living. Don't underestimate the power of that revelation. Don't underestimate the things young men will wager in order to play that game one more time (*War*, pp. 144-45).

Following are the personal memoirs of three veterans:

Philip Caputo. *A Rumor of War* (New York: Ballantine Books, 1977). Caputo narrates his experience as an infantry officer in Viet Nam in 1965-66 and describes his return as a newspaper correspondent covering the American exodus a decade later.

Brian Castner. *The Long Walk: A Story of War and the Life that Follows* (New York: Anchor Books, 2013). This narrative is based on Castner's three tours of duty in the Middle East.

Tim O'Brien. *The Things They Carried* (New York: Broadway Books, 1990). The linked short stories in this book recount the experiences of an infantry company in Viet Nam. The book is labeled fiction, but the stories are based on O'Brien's experience, and he gives his protagonist his own name. He writes that "story-truth is truer sometimes than happening-truth" (p. 179).

These three books are equally relevant to the discussion of post-traumatic stress disorder and moral injury, below.

Post-traumatic Stress Disorder and Moral Injury

After years of railing at the inadequacy of "post-traumatic stress disorder" in describing the suffering of Alan Morris and other veterans, I discovered authors who recognize the disorder as a "moral injury"—the effect of being caught up in action that violates one's sense of what is right. The veterans have been victims, and some, perpetrators, and the resulting injury is to the soul.

Most enlightening are the writings of two psychiatrists—Jonathan Shay and Bessel van der Kolk, who have spent decades treating Vietnam veterans. Lt. Col. Dave Grossman brings experience as an army Ranger and paratrooper and his work as a psychology professor at West Point. I also recommend a book by two divinity school professors and ethicists, Rita Nakashima Brock and Gabriella Lettini.

Jonathan Shay. *Achilles in Vietnam: Combat Trauma and the Undoing of Character.* New York: Scribner, 1994.

_____. *Odysseus in America: Combat Trauma and the Trials of Homecoming.* New York: Scribner, 2002.

> We do not refer to a veteran who has had an arm blown off by a grenade as suffering from "Missing Arm Disorder." But I am not going to fight it. "PTSD" it is, even though I much prefer "psychological injury." Combat PTSD is a war injury. Veterans with combat PTSD are war wounded, carrying the burdens of sacrifice for the rest of us as surely as the amputees, the burned, the blind, and the paralyzed carry them. [There is a] distinction between simple PTSD—the persistence into civilian life of adaptations necessary to survive battle—and complex PTSD, which is simple PTSD plus the destruction of the capacity for social trust (*Odysseus in America*, p. 4).

Bessel A. van der Kolk. *The Body Keeps the Score: Brain, Mind, and Body in the Healing of Trauma.* New York: Viking Penguin, 2014.

Many treatment approaches for traumatic stress focus on desensitizing patients to their past, with the expectation that re-exposure to their traumas will reduce emotional outbursts and flashbacks. I believe that this is based on a misunderstanding of what happens in traumatic stress. We must most of all help our patients to live fully and securely in the present. In order to do that, we need to help bring those brain structures that deserted them when they were overwhelmed by trauma back. Desensitization may make you less reactive, but if you cannot feel satisfaction in ordinary everyday things like taking a walk, cooking a meal, or playing with your kids, life will pass you by (p. 73).

Lt. Col. Dave Grossman. *On Killing: The Psychological Cost of Learning to Kill in War and Society.* New York: Little, Brown, 1st ed. 1995, rev. ed. 2009.

When a soldier shoots a child who is throwing a grenade the child's weapon explodes, and there is only the mutilated body left to rationalize. There is no convenient weapon indisputably telling the world of the victim's lethality and the killer's innocence; there is only a dead child, speaking mutely of horror and innocence lost. The innocence of childhood, soldiers, and nations, all lost in a single act reenacted countless times for ten endless years until a weary nation finally retreats in horror and dismay from its long nightmare (p. 269).

Rita Nakashima Brock and Gabriella Lettini. *Soul Repair: Recovering from Moral Injury after War.* Boston: Beacon Press, 2012.

The consequences of violating one's conscience, even if the act was unavoidable or seemed right at the time, can be devastating. Responses include overwhelming depression, guilt, and self-medication through alcohol or drugs. Moral injury can lead veterans to feelings of worthlessness, remorse, and despair; they may feel as if they lost their souls in combat and are no longer who they were. Connecting emotionally to others becomes impossible for those trapped inside the walls of such feelings. When the consequences become overwhelming, the only relief may seem to be to leave this life behind (pp. xv-xvi).

Edward Tick's Journeys of Healing and Reconciliation

Edward Tick is a psychotherapist who has devoted over four decades to healing the wounds of war. Each year since 2000 he has taken to Viet Nam a small group, typically no more than a dozen, veterans and loved ones of both veterans and war dead. These journeys are scheduled intentionally so that the travelers will be in

Viet Nam on U.S. Veterans Day, November 11. The travelers are not tourists. They are on journeys of healing and reconciliation, the fruit of all Edward Tick has come to know about war and warriors, and about the differences between PTSD and moral injury on the one hand, and on the other what Tick refers to as "Soldier's Heart," which is also the name he has given his non-profit organization. See soldiersheart.net I traveled as part of his small group who were in Viet Nam on Veterans Day in 2018, and I wrote the Afterword to this book while still there.

Edward Tick is not only a healer but also a writer whose books share both the depth of his understanding and the power of his vision.

Edward Tick. *Warrior's Return: Restoring the Soul After War.* Boulder, CO: Sounds True, 2014.

> The wound that today we call PTSD may not be primarily to the individual but to the body politic, the nation's soul. ... We expend much time, effort, and resources on symptoms. We diagnose, then attempt to eradicate or control them. We thus overload individual vets with responsibility for their own suffering and miss the full portrait of war. We do not treat war's invisible wounds effectively because for many reasons we do not understand them accurately. We have inherited the trance and denial, what Robert McNamara called "the fog of war." The misinterpretations of our times prevent us from seeing what is in front of us (p. 36).

...

We tend to focus on American veterans and casualties, trying to stitch together our own broken people and society. But limiting our scope misleads us. ... War ... causes wounding to the deepest dimensions of our humanity. These wounds carry pain that will not and should not go away. In this sense the invisible wound is not a negative, certainly not a disease. ... The wound is proof that as a result of war we will be different forever. It is also proof of our humanity, that we are caring, vulnerable people who cannot go through zones of hell with impunity and cannot harm others without harming ourselves (p. 56).

...

When we think of the invisible wound ... as a communal and spiritual wound that we all share and for which we are all responsible, we love and support, listen to, engage, and restore survivors, work together with them to repair our wounded world and live together in empathy.

...

War healing requires a spiritual approach because war is Leviathan and trauma is a deep, devastating, and enduring soul wound. It requires a restorative rather than reparative psychological approach because a moral journey must be completed, the identity must be re-created, meaning must be discovered, and spirit must be renewed. It requires a communal approach because it is a social disorder resulting from neglecting and isolating warriors and not fulfilling our social contract and because the citizens did not initiate their warriors. It requires an archetypal approach because the individual's story must be joined to the stories of the ages and to the universal and eternal patterns in these stories (p. 161-2).

_____. *War and the Soul: Healing Our Nation's Veterans from Post-traumatic Stress Disorder.* Wheaton, IL: Quest Books, Theosophical Publishing House, 2005.

The numbers of Vietnamese people killed, wounded, missing, displaced, homeless, and disabled during the Vietnam War far exceeded ours. Their ecology and infra-structure were ravaged, while ours was untouched. How disarming it is, then, for Americans to find Vietnamese welcoming them as honored guests and offering friend-ship and forgiveness – while many at home still quake in terror of how we might be treated around the world.

Viet Nam is a society characterized by a tight and complex kinship system. While American veterans have no such system at home, the Vietnamese welcome everyone, even American veterans. No one is blamed. All are forgiven. [The Vietnamese] receive our veterans as lost brothers and sisters with whom they share histo]ry and their most influential life experiences. It is in such company, and before such audiences, where relationship and honor are significant, that initiation is recognized and healing occurs (p. 268).

_____. *The Golden Tortoise: Journeys in Viet Nam*. Los Angeles: Red Hen Press, 2005.

We have never for a single lifetime, never for a span of generations, known a sustained peace. Nor have many of us attained that state of inner peace we long for. We do not know what comes after the killing fields. We may not even know what peace is.

War is always life gone wrong. I wonder, as do many survivors – will I ever cleanse my deep accumulated pain and grief from old battles and their losses. Can we be free of the anguish at life having gone wrong? How do we meet and talk with others when it was war that first introduced us, war that drenched our minds, relationships, and countries in a poison as deadly to the soul as Agent Orange is to body and land?

I yearn for a peace beyond the sheathing of swords. I return to Viet Nam to seek and learn of this peace (p. 81).

I recommend another book by Edward Tick as well.

_____. *The Practice of Dream Healing: Bringing Ancient Greek Mysteries into Modern Medicine.* Wheaton, IL: Quest Books, Theosophical Publishing House, 2001.

The Anti-War Movement During the Vietnam War and the Killings at Kent State

The events before, during, and after the May 4, 1970, National Guard killings at Kent State provide a clear lens for viewing and interpreting the anti-war movement. The most incisive account is by Peter Davies, who spent several years researching in support of the litigation on behalf of the wounded students and the families of the dead. Thomas Hensley, then a Kent State political science professor, discusses his and his graduate students' research into how the litigation affected public attitudes about the killings. Thomas Grace, a student wounded on May 4, and a friend of Alan Morris, became a professor of history. His heavily documented book overturns the myth of Kent as a sleepy Midwestern college town where there was no reason to predict any significant anti-war activity.

Peter Davies. *The Truth about Kent State: A Challenge to the American Conscience.* New York: Farrar, Straus, Giroux, 1973.

Now it appears that what was initially reported to be wild, indiscriminate shooting on the part of some thirty ill-trained and frightened young Ohio National Guardsmen may well have been a premeditated barrage by about ten experienced, riot-trained guardsmen, with the remaining troops firing in reaction. The gunfire claimed the lives of four students hundreds of feet away. They died as the result of an explosion of emotions incited by exactly the kind of rhetoric on the part of Ohio's political and military leaders which President Nixon had found so undesirable during his campaign for election. Nine other students were wounded. One was paralyzed and another maimed. It was an event of tragic proportion, but what happened afterward is the real tragedy of Kent State (pp. 2-3).

Thomas R. Hensley, *The Kent State Incident: Impact of Judicial Process on Public Attitudes*. Westport, CT: Greenwood Press, 1981.

The words "Kent State" hold a singular meaning in the minds of most Americans. A large but relatively unknown university in northeast Ohio gains instant worldwide attention during a thirteen second span on May 4, 1970, when Ohio National Guardsmen killed four Kent State University students and wounded nine others. From that moment in history Kent State was to be thought of not only as an institution of higher education but also as the place

where the agony of a country divided over
the Vietnam War crystalized in a manner
that left the entire country shocked and
embittered (p. 4).

Thomas M. Grace, *Kent State: Death and Dissent
in the Long Sixties*. Amherst and Boston: University of
Massachusetts Press, 2016.

The battle over the meaning and memory of
May 4 began almost as soon as the shooting
stopped. We've seen that as news of the
killings at Kent State University spread in
May 1970, outraged students throughout
the country went on strike to protest the
violent suppression of peaceful dissent,
while countless other people expressed the
view that Kent's protestors only got what
they deserved. In many ways these two
reactions framed the subsequent debate:
Were the casualties a deliberate act of
injustice that must be remembered in order
to be rectified? Were these young people
unarmed combatants in a war to stop a
war? And were the students themselves
primarily responsible for what happened—
the killings an object lesson in what happens
when dissent turns into confrontation? Or
was it all just a tragic mistake (like the war
itself, as some believed), leaving wounds
that could only be healed through acts of
reconciliation (p. 267)?

These two books provide unvarnished exposés: Joseph Kelner and James Munves. *The Kent State Coverup.* New York: Harper & Row, 1980. This is an insider's view of the initial civil litigation in federal court in which the wounded students and the families of those killed were plaintiffs. Joseph Kelner served as their chief counsel.

I.F. Stone. *The Killings at Kent State: How Murder Went Unpunished.* New York: Vintage, 1971. This includes the Justice Department's secret summary of FBI findings and the Portage County Grand Jury Report of the events of May 4 and the preceding weekend.

I wrote my "Open Letter to a Vietnam Veteran" as a term paper in a class taught by Walter Capps, California legislator and professor of religious studies. I conclude this section of recommended readings with selections from the book he edited and the one he authored as well as selections from a unique collection of interviews by Joan Morrison and Robert K. Morrison. Those quoted from Capps' *The Vietnam Reader* are Todd Gitlin, who in 1970 was a leader of the Students for a Democratic Society (SDS), and James Quay, a conscientious objector during the Vietnam War.

Walter Capps, ed. *The Vietnam Reader.* New York: Routledge, 1991.

[I]t's the so-called conservatives ... who give the antiwar movement credit. They firmly believe that the country was seized during the '60s by a "new class" of overeducated left intellectuals, tantrum-throwing students, media liberals, uppity minorities, feminists, hedonists, homosexuals, and assorted bleeding hearts, who not only succeeded in trashing tradition, standards, the family, and all natural hierarchy, but also broke the back of national security, leveling America's just position in the world and costing us an achievable and noble victory in Vietnam. They have spent the past ten years trying to figure out how to recapture lost terrain from the barbarians. And they are haunted by the specter of revived antiwar activity—for good reason. For despite their paranoid exaggerations and their self-serving refusal to acknowledge just how much ideological ground they have already reconquered, they know in their bones what many veterans of the '60s don't know or have forgotten: that the movement against the Vietnam War was history's most successful movement against a shooting war. — Todd Gitlin, "The Achievements of the War-protest Movement" (pp. 157-58).

Opposition to killing must begin before the war begins. The crucial moment in the passage from civilian life to military life is called "induction." The word comes from the Latin meaning "to be led into." At a certain point, you are asked to take a step forward. You can't be forced to take that step and no matter how many others step forward with you, it is a step only you can take or refuse to take. Once you take that step you enter a world where you are expected to obey all lawful commands given to you, no matter what your personal objections might be. I can understand the courage that it takes to obey, especially when you consider that such obedience might ultimately cost you your life. That is the step I refused to take. While I felt my country had the right to require service of me, I denied it the right to order me to kill other human beings. That is a step I hope that all of us might one day refuse to take. — James Quay, "Life, Liberty, and the Right to Protest" (p. 212).

Walter H. Capps. *The Unfinished War: Vietnam and the American Conscience*, 2nd ed. Boston: Beacon Press, 1982.

The Vietnam War was problematic nearly from the first because it lacked effective moral and metaphysical supports. ... Those who fought in the war were not easily able to explain why they were there, and the battle cries they had been taught did not provide convincing validation. Since direct United States involvement ended in 1975 with no lasting resolution of the fundamental dilemma and without satisfactory military closure, the debate has continued about the propriety of our actions. Nearly everyone views the war as an enormous national tragedy, but there are still great differences of opinion regarding precisely wherein that tragedy lies. One side continues to believe that military objectives were prematurely foreshortened by the social, psychological, and political confusion and consternation at home. The other side tends to believe that the upheaval at home stands as valid and compelling testimony that, from the start, the war effort was a mistake: the United States had no real business being there (p. 168).

Joan Morrison and Robert K. Morrison, in *From Camelot to Kent State: The Sixties Experience in the Words of Those Who Lived It* (New York: Times Books, 1987), quote William Sloan Coffin, the Yale Chaplain and prominent anti-war activist, and Philip Berrigan, the Catholic priest who, with his brother Daniel, became the voices of Roman Catholic opposition to the war.

When I opposed the government, it was in the name of my country—in the name of American ideals. It was always a lovers' quarrel, not a grudge fight. My patriotic fervor has always been at a very high pitch, second only to, I hope, my very deep Christian convictions. I was never tempted, for instance, to go to Canada or leave the country, but I was sympathetic to the feelings of those who did. I remember once after addressing the Yale alumni in Buffalo during the Vietnam War, a doctor who had me in tow asked me what I wanted to do, and I said, "I'd love to see Niagara Falls at night." So we went over there, and you know it's better from the Canadian side, so we went across the border, and suddenly I said to him. "Stop. Let me out." And he did. And I just burst into tears out of this overwhelming sense of relief at being outside of America for fifteen minutes. I hadn't realized what a burden it was during the war in Vietnam to be an American. — William Sloan Coffin (p. 106).

I was morally outraged by the escalation in Vietnam. I was ashamed that we would be doing something like this, because I had believed in the history books, and I expected better of our country. Here we were, a superpower, you know, chewing up an agrarian society—a bunch of peasants in black pajamas. And then you'd see the young soldiers in uniform in bus stations and train stations and airports when you traveled along, and you knew that they were being used and that it was wrong. Some of them questioned the war and didn't want to be sent to Vietnam. They had sense enough to say, "No, this isn't right. And if I go along, I'm liable to come home in a tin box." And others were gung-ho for the war. They were all victims. They were eighteen, nineteen years old, babes in the woods. —Philip Berrigan (pp. 145-46).

Jungian Psychology, Analysis, and Dream Work

Following are selected classic texts and more contemporary expressions and applications of Jungian thought:

Jung, Carl G., ed. *Man and His Symbols.* New York: Dell, 1964. Jung presents his life's work in psychology for a general audience. He examines the unconscious, especially its language of symbols as expressed in dreams.

Jung, C.G. *Memories, Dreams, Reflections*, rev. ed. Aniela Jaffé. New York: Vintage, 1989. This classic is Jung's life story as he told it to his colleague Aniela Jaffé.

_____. *The Red Book,* ed. Sonu Shamdasani. New York: W.W. Norton, 2009. From 1913 to 1930, Jung confronted his own unconscious and developed a method of translating emotions into images that he called "active imagination." He later copied his reflections and his intricate paintings into the book *Liber Novus ("Red Book")*, which was bound in red leather. This Reader's Edition does not include the paintings.

Slattery, Dennis Patrick. *Bridge Work: Essays on Mythology, Literature and Psychology.* Carpenteria, CA: Mandorla Books, 2015. Slattery, my former student, has recently retired from his position on the core faculty in the Mythological Studies, Depth Psychology, and Depth Psychotherapy programs at Pacifica Graduate Institute. This book includes essays entitled "Dante's *Terza Rima* in *The Divine Comedy:* The Road of Therapy" (pp. 25-45), and "The Confluence of Remembering and Forgetting" (pp. 149-63), which are relevant to Jungian analysis.

Taylor, Jeremy. *Dream Work: Techniques for Discovering the Creative Power in Dreams.* New York: Paulist Press, 1983. Taylor taught the dream work class I took in seminary. We put his techniques to work, and some of us still apply them to our great benefit.

von Franz, Marie-Louise. *Projection and Recollection in Jungian Psychology: Reflections of the Soul.* Chicago: Open Court, 1980. von Franz worked with Jung for three decades and became an analyst herself. This book presents all the major concepts involved in Jungian psychology.

Wikman, Monika R. *The Pregnant Darkness: Alchemy and the Rebirth of Consciousness.* York Beach, ME: Nicolas Hays, 2004. Wikman is a Jungian analyst. Her book describes psychoanalysis using the metaphor of the alchemical process that I use throughout this book.

_____. *Using Alchemical Archetypes in Jungian Analysis.* Shrink Rap Radio podcast #235. www.shrinkrapradio.com/2010/04/24/235a

Poetry and the Search for Meaning

Here are the poetry collections from which poems quoted in this book are taken, along with some discussions of the poetry:

Berry, Wendell. "Three Elegiac Poems," *Collected Poems of Wendell Berry (1957-1882).* San Francisco: North Point Press, 1985, pp. 49, 51.

Hall, H. Palmer. *From the Periphery: Poems and Essays.* San Antonio: Chili Verde Press, 1994.

Klepfisz, Irena. "Dedications to *Bashert*," *Poems to Live by in Troubling Times*, ed. Joan Murray. Boston: Beacon Press, 2006, pp. 14-18.

McTaggart, Ursula. "Artistry & Activism: The Poetry of Irene Klepfisz," *Solidarity* (http://www. solidarity-us.org/site/print/527).

Pacernick, Gary. *Meaning and Memory: Interviews with Fourteen Jewish Poets*. Columbus: Ohio State University Press, 2001.

Rich, Adrienne. "Transcendental Etude," *The Dream of a Common Language: Poems, 1974-1977*. New York: W.W. Norton, 1978, p. 72.

Sources Cited in the Text

Chinnery, Philip D. "Phil Marshall Had One of the Most Dangerous Jobs in Vietnam – Flying a Dust-off Medevac Chopper," *Vietnam*, October 1994, pp. 10, 56.

Doyle, Brian. "Well, Some of It Was True," *American Scholar*. Summer 2016, pp. 98, 103.

Ellsberg, Daniel. *Secrets: A Memoir of Vietnam and the Pentagon Papers*. New York: Viking Press, 2002.

Freeman, Aaron. "Planning Ahead Can Make a Difference in the End," *All Things Considered*, National Public Radio, June 1, 2005.

Greenberg, Gary. "Who Are You Calling Crazy?" *The Sun*, July 2016, pp. 4, 13.

Mason, Patience H.C. *Recovering from the War: A Woman's Guide to Helping Your Vietnam Vet, Your Family, and Yourself.* New York: Viking Press, 1990.

Milgrom, Jo. *Handmade Midrash: Workshops in Visual Theology*. Philadelphia, New York, and Jerusalem: The Jewish Publication Society, 1992/5752.

Pagels, Elaine. *The Gnostic Gospels.* New York: Vintage, 1979.

Pentagon Papers, The: The Defense Department History of United States Decisionmaking on Vietnam, Senator Gravel Edition. Boston: Beacon Press, 1971.

Sheehan, Neil. "Vietnam Archive: Pentagon Study Traces 3 Decades of Growing U.S. Involvement," *The New York Times*, June 13, 1971.

Zaleski, Jeff. "To Feel the Love: A Conversation with Barry Svigals," *Parabola*, Fall 2016, pp. 10-19.

About the Author

Barbara Child's first retirement came in 1978 when she gave up her position as tenured English professor at Kent State University after 15 years there, teaching nearly every kind of writing course anybody ever thought of—essay writing, poetry writing, fiction writing, and  eventually legal writing. She left to practice poverty law as an attorney with the Legal Services Corporation, then went back to academia to teach in law schools, first at Golden Gate University in San Francisco where she served as Director of Writing and Research and then at University of Florida where she created the position of Director of Legal Drafting.

She advocated drafting legal documents in plain language and taught this approach in workshops for state legislative drafting bureaus through the National Conference of State Legislatures. The second edition of her textbook, *Drafting Legal Documents,* is still in use over two decades after its publication.

When Barbara left academia in 1993 after 15 years in law, that was her second retirement. She left to go to seminary. A Unitarian Universalist, she became an Accredited Interim Minister, and she retired for the third time when she completed her last full-time interim ministry in 2010. Since then the second edition of *In the Interim: Strategies for Interim Ministers and Congregations* was published, edited by Barbara and Keith Kron. Forthcoming in 2019 will be the collection of readings and rituals she has edited for congregations in times of change and transition.

Barbara does not anticipate any more retirements. She continues to mentor ministers and serve congregations as short-term consultant. She lives in her log cabin in the woods of Brown County, outside the small artists' colony of Nashville, Indiana. She expects to die a long time from now, either composing editorial notes at the computer or pausing for the next thought with a pen in her hand.